Sorry I Was Busy Scrolling

Focus Tips For When Your Brain Is Addicted To Notifications

I.L. Hartley

Published by

Deckademy Pty Td

Pen Tillman

Tillman Forsyth Publishing House

tillmanforsythpublishings@gmail.com

v.1.0.04

This page is intentionally left blank.

Keep Scrolling

Table of Contents

Author's Note:

First of all, high-five. If you're reading this, it means you either:

> a) actually finished Book 1 (legend),
>
> b) skimmed Book 1 and jumped straight here because the cover promised more coffee and less judgment (also valid), or
>
> c) bought this book on impulse while doom-scrolling at 2:47 a.m. and are now wondering why your phone is still winning.

Any of those is a win. Write it down. We're counting it.

If you have joined us from Book 1, welcome back! If you're new here, well, enjoy it while you can, welcome to the club, towels on the left.

Here's the deal: I'm still not a productivity guru.

I still don't wake up at 4:00 a.m. to do anything except regret waking up at 4:00 a.m.

I still own mismatched socks, a laundry pile that occasionally sends me passive-aggressive vibes, and a phone that behaves like a needy toddler who discovered sugar and the word "why."

But the toddler has upgraded.

These days it doesn't just interrupt me—it hijacks entire afternoons.

I've lost whole chapters of this book to threads about whether hot chips are better with aioli or gravy (spoiler: both are correct and I still don't know why I needed 47 minutes to decide).

I've set "Do Not Disturb" only to immediately turn it off because "what if it's important this time?"

It never is.

It's always a like on a photo of my lunch from three weeks ago.

This book is still a **No-Judgment Zone.**

The stories here are true-ish still (names changed to protect the equally addicted). The tips, though? They're painfully real.

These are the sneaky little rebellions I had to invent after Book 1 taught me how to start… but left me defenceless when the notifications arrived like uninvited guests who brought their own snacks and wouldn't leave.

We're not aiming for monk-mode perfection in these pages.

We're not deleting apps, going grayscale forever, or moving to a cabin with no Wi-Fi (although I've Googled it at 3 a.m. more times than I'd like to admit).

We're aiming for "I now lose twenty minutes instead of two hours."

We're aiming for "I can stay in the thing long enough to finish it… most of the time."

We're aiming for slightly better than yesterday, even when the dopamine slot machine in my pocket is trying very hard to convince me otherwise.

If you've already wasted half the day scrolling, don't worry.

The second half is still up for grabs, as we learned (hopefully) in Book 1.

And if your brain is currently screaming "but there might be something funny/important/validating in the next swipe," that's okay too.

We're going to work with that brain, not against it.

So, grab your coffee, put the phone face-down for just a second (I believe in you), and let's figure out how to make the glowing rectangle a reluctant sidekick instead of the boss of your afternoon.

Stay messy.

Stay curious.

Stay moving (even if it's just one less refresh at a time).

— *I.L. Hartley*

Recovering Chronic Scroller

P.S I will say that some of these chapters will be perfect for you, whilst others you will not be able to relate to. There's no one-size-fits-all magic glove that fits. I will say though, in this place you may not know your size at all – so stay with me, try your best, and let's get fitted together.

Introduction: The Notification Vortex

If you're reading this at 2:47 p.m. on a Sunday while after conquering the work week, feeling refreshed and rejuvenated enjoying some down time, then well done. Please leave. This book isn't for you.

I joke, of course, but hey if that really is you then be proud. Be even more proud if you're at this stage now after being categorized as one of our superstars from Chapter 1 of Book 1 (if you've read it – if not then look it up because I can't be bothered explaining it here.)

If this isn't you, and you're still fighting those distractions and have joined us from Book 1 or a newcomer who also wants to hear about others suffering (because let's be honest – sometimes we feel a little less pain when we know others are in the same pain), then I give you a warm welcome.

For those who read Book 1, please tell me your weeks have started to be come a little bit better. You survived the Half-Day Trap (hopefully?).

You even managed a few 5-Minute Rebellions and probably crossed off at least one of your Three Things without turning it into a four-hour perfection spiral (maybe?)

Give yourself a quiet high-five. That's real progress. If not, then don't worry, keep trying and keep pushing. The act of attempting will soon turn into the act of doing.

For those who need a recap, or those who never read it – Book 1 was about salvaging the second half of the day when the first half had already slipped through your fingers.

We learned to forgive the wasted morning, fake the start with five pathetic minutes, shrink the to-do list to three non-negotiable wins, and give ourselves permission to ship "good enough" instead of waiting for perfection.

It worked (mostly).

You probably got more done than you expected on at least a few Tuesdays.

But here's the part we didn't talk about enough:

Even when you start… you can't stay.

The moment momentum builds, something— anything—whispers *"hey, look over here for just a second,"* and flow turns into scatter, deep work turns into shallow dopamine hits, and the afternoon evaporates into a collage of half-finished thoughts and other people's highlight reels.

This book is for that exact moment.

It's not about becoming one of those terrifying digital-minimalist monks who only check email once a week on an iPad, with their phone being shut off since 2015, while meditating in complete silence.

This is about staying in the room with your actual life for longer than five minutes at a time—no matter what tries to pull you out.

It's about turning the phone, the tabs, the "brilliant ideas," the interruptions, and all the other shiny distractions from the boss of your attention into reluctant, slightly sulky sidekicks that occasionally do what you ask.

It's about reclaiming the focus you already fought so hard to start.

The Distraction Vortex (Yes, It Has Layers):

We've all been sold a polite lie: that productivity is mostly about time management.

Get up earlier, block your calendar, use the right app, eat the frog, drink the green juice.

If you just organized better, you'd win.

But most of us aren't losing time to poor planning anymore.

We're losing it to engineered (and accidental) distraction.

The average person switches tasks or checks something every 3–11 minutes depending on who you ask.

Each switch costs you—on average—23 minutes to get back into whatever you were doing before.

Do the maths: that's hours.

Hours of your life vacuumed up by variable rewards, infinite tabs, social proof, FOMO, sudden curiosity spikes, people who think "quick question" means "let's rebuild the entire strategy," and the quiet terror that if you don't look / check / research / reply right now, you'll miss something important/validating/funny/outrageous.

Your brain isn't weak.

It's just running modern software on hardware that hasn't had a meaningful update since we stopped worrying about leopards in the tall grass. We covered this in the first book, but we like to run it back.

Back then, novelty = survival.

New rustle in the bushes? Pay attention or die.

Today, new rustle = new like / new tab / new idea / new email subject line in bold.

Same wiring.

Different stakes.

The vortex isn't random.

Parts of it are designed.

Parts of it are self-inflicted.

Either way, it's winning because it's faster, louder, and has been optimized by several billion dollars of A/B testing plus our own very human desire to feel connected, informed, entertained, and not-bored for more than thirty seconds.

And here's the part that stings:

You're not above it.

I'm not above it.

Nobody is above it.

The people who seem to have perfect focus either have a different dopamine baseline (lucky them), have outsourced the battle to extreme systems, or are lying on Instagram about how productive they are.

Most of us are in the middle:

We want to get stuff done.

We like some parts of the digital world (music, quick photos of funny signs, memes that make us snort-laugh at our desk).

But we hate how easily it turns a productive afternoon into a collage of half-finished thoughts and other people's lives.

The good news?

Understanding the vortex—all its layers—is half the rebellion.

Once you see the slot machine, the open-tab graveyard, the interruption bait, and the shiny-idea trap for what they are, you stop feeling morally defective every time you lose forty minutes.

You start seeing it as a game you can play better—not by refusing to play, but by changing the rules so the house doesn't always win.

This book isn't about "out-willpower-ing" every distraction on Earth. That's a mug's game.

It's about out-smarting them.

A little bit. One tiny defence at a time.

We're going to build fences around your attention without turning your life into a monastery.

We're going to make starting easier to protect (because Book 1 already taught you how to start).

We're going to turn the phone, the tabs, the interruptions, the sudden urges, and all the other attention thieves into tools you control instead of forces that control you.

The only rule in these pages is the same one from Book 1: Forgive yourself for the last ninety-two minutes (or ninety-two days).

You cannot build focused afternoons on a foundation of shame. Shame is heavy. It's hard to stay in flow when you're lugging it around.

So, take a breath.

Put the phone face-down for just a second (I believe in you).

Close three of those tabs (you know the ones).

The vortex is loud, but it's not unbeatable.

And the second half of your day—your actual life—is still waiting.

Let's stop apologizing for getting distracted and start training the distractions to sit.

Let's go.

PART 1: WHY YOUR BRAIN LOVES THE SCROLL MORE THAN YOU

Chapter 1: The Attention Economy Is Rigged (And You're The Product)

You're going to see a certain theme with the way I write. I said it in the other book as a shortform disclaimer, but I write less instructive and more conversationally.

I feel that, just for me personally, it is the best way for me to communicate, so forgive me for the anecdotes and drifting, and stay with me; there are some juicy treasures buried in this garden of ramblings, I promise. Anyway, I digress…

It's 11:14 a.m. on a Wednesday that already feels like it owes you money. You've finally sat down—after the usual morning dance of coffee, emails, and telling yourself *"today's the day"*—with the laptop open to the one task that actually matters: that client proposal / tax return / first chapter of the thing you've been promising yourself for two years.

The cursor blinks. You take a breath. You type the first sentence. It's not Shakespeare, but it's something. Momentum is building. You're actually doing the thing. And then the phone buzzes.

Not a siren. Not your mum. Not even a real human.

Just a gentle, polite vibration that says: "*Hey… someone reacted to your comment from last week.*" You glance over. You tell yourself: "*One second. Literally one second to see what the comment is.*" You pick up the phone.

You unlock it. Seventeen minutes later you're distracted again, laughing alone at your desk like a lunatic, while the proposal document is still sitting there with one lonely sentence and a blinking cursor that now feels like it's judging you. Sound familiar?

Of course it does.

Because that exact sequence has happened to every person reading this book at least once this week. Probably twice.

I've done it more times than I care to count.

I once lost entire mornings researching office chairs, because when I sat down in my office chair I felt a slight kink in my lower back and thought to myself "*hmmm… I should do something about that – I wonder if it's the chair? Do I need a new one?"* This is a true story, by the way.

Spoiler: I still sit on the same broken IKEA chair from years ago.

I didn't buy a new chair.

I did, however, get distracted easily.

Why?

Why does a grown adult with actual responsibilities suddenly need to know the difference between tilt tension and synchro-tilt mechanisms at 11:17 a.m.?

Why does the brain go from "let's write the damn proposal" to "I wonder if my posture is secretly killing me" in under ninety seconds?

Because the game is rigged.

Not against you personally.

Not because you're weak, undisciplined, or secretly addicted to cat videos (although… maybe a little).

It's rigged against every single one of us who owns a smartphone, opens a browser, or has ever clicked "Allow Notifications" because the pop-up made it sound like refusing would end world peace.

Your attention is the most valuable real estate on the planet right now.

Tech companies aren't selling you ads.

They're selling your eyeballs, your time, your micro-moments of focus to the highest bidder.

Every ping, every infinite scroll, every autoplay video, every "recommended for you" thumbnail is a tiny, perfectly engineered hook designed to keep you pulling the lever just one more time.

And the house always wins.

I used to think I was just bad at focus.

I'd beat myself up after every lost hour: *"Why can't I just sit down and do the thing? Why am I like this?"*

Then I realized the truth: I'm not failing at focus.

I'm succeeding at exactly what a multi-billion-dollar industry spent years training me to succeed at.

I'm an excellent, high-performing customer of the attention economy.

I give them my time reliably, predictably, and in ever-increasing amounts.

If distraction was an Olympic sport, most of us would have gold medals hanging in our home offices right next to the unpaid bills.

The funny part?

The moment you see the casino for what it is, you stop feeling like a loser every time you lose a hand.

You stop thinking "I'm broken" and start thinking *"oh… I've been playing poker with people who know the deck is marked."*

That shift is the first quiet rebellion of this book.

We're not going to pretend you can walk out of the casino forever.

(You still need the phone for maps, music, texting your mum, and pretending to look busy when someone walks past your desk.)

We're just going to teach you how to play a slightly different game—one where you keep more of your chips, lose fewer afternoons, and maybe even walk away with something that feels like a win.

So, if you're sitting there right now with too many tabs open, a half-written sentence, and a vague sense that you've been robbed…

you have been.

But the robbery isn't random.

It's systematic.

And once you understand the system, you stop being such an easy mark.

Let's pull back the curtain on how the attention economy actually works.

No guilt. No lectures. Just the truth, with a side of "yeah… I've done that too."

Ready to see how deep the rabbit hole goes?

(And yes, I promise we won't spend the next hour researching rabbit holes. We've all been there.)

Let's call it what it is: your attention is currently the most valuable commodity on the planet.

Here's the simplest version:

Tech platforms don't primarily sell you products or services.

They sell you — or at least tiny slices of your time and focus — to advertisers who want to sell you actual products and services.

Okay, let's stop dancing around the edges and look at the actual machinery that keeps us glued to screens when we'd rather be doing literally anything else.

I'm not going to hit you with a 47-slide PowerPoint of tech-bro jargon.

I'm going to show you the handful of simple, sneaky tricks that turn a harmless rectangle into the most effective attention thief in human history.

These aren't accidents.

They're features.

And once you can name them, you start spotting them everywhere — which is the first step to not letting them own your afternoon.

Variable Rewards – The Slot-Machine Heartbeat

Remember those old casino machines that spit out coins at unpredictable intervals?

That's the gold standard of addiction engineering.

You pull the lever, you don't know if you'll get nothing, a small win, or the jackpot.

The uncertainty is what keeps you pulling.

Your phone does exactly the same thing, except the "coins" are likes, replies, funny memes, breaking news, or that one friend who finally texted back after three days.

Every refresh, every swipe, every notification is a pull.

Most of the time you get nothing.

Sometimes you get a tiny dopamine sprinkle.

Every now and then you hit the jackpot — a viral comment, a message from someone you actually like, a video that makes you snort-laugh so hard you almost drop your coffee.

That unpredictability is why "just one more scroll" turns into forty-seven more.

I've pulled the lever at 2 a.m. wondering if the next post will finally make me feel less alone, only to realise I've been staring at strangers arguing about whether pineapple belongs on pizza for an hour.

The slot machine doesn't care about my existential crisis.

It just knows I'll keep pulling.

Infinite Scroll – No Natural Off-Ramp

Old websites had a bottom.

You reached page 12, it said "no more results," and your brain got the signal: "Okay, we're done here."

Modern feeds have no bottom.

They just keep loading.

No edge.

No finish line.

Your brain never gets the little "task complete" ping it evolved to love.

So, it keeps going, waiting for closure that never arrives.

I once scrolled Instagram until my thumb cramped, looking for the end like it was a level in a video game.

There is no end.

There is only more.

And more is always just one flick away.

Social Proof & FOMO – The "Everyone Else Is Winning" Trap

Your brain still cares deeply about belonging and status — leftovers from when being left out of the tribe meant death by exposure or lions.

Today, that same wiring sees likes, stories, followers, and perfectly filtered lives and whispers: *"They're all doing better than you. You're missing out. Check again."*

It's not vanity.

It's ancient survival software misfiring in a world of curated highlight reels.

I've caught myself comparing my messy desk and lukewarm coffee to someone's sunrise yoga in Bali and felt genuinely worse about my life for about thirty seconds.

Then I remembered: they probably took 47 photos to get that one perfect shot, and right now they're also sitting in traffic arguing with their mum on the phone.

But the algorithm doesn't show me that part.

It shows me the filtered version — and my brain buys the lie.

Autoplay & Algorithmic Curation – It Knows You Better Than You Do

You watch one video about office chair fails.

Suddenly the next one starts automatically.

Then another.

Then a compilation.

Then a "people are awesome" montage.

You didn't choose any of it.

The algorithm chose for you — based on what kept you watching last time, last week, last year.

It's like having a very attentive but slightly creepy friend who finishes your sentences and always suggests exactly what will keep you in the room.

I've gone from *"I'll just watch one quick clip"* to *"how am I watching people restore vintage tools at 3 a.m.?"*

I didn't search for vintage tool restoration.

The algorithm decided I needed it.

And it was right — I watched for forty minutes.

That's how good it is.

Intermittent Reinforcement – The Occasional Jackpot

This is the cruelest one.

If every pull gave you nothing, you'd stop.

If every pull gave you a win, you'd get bored.

But when wins are random and rare — just often enough to keep hope alive — you become almost impossible to shake.

That one friend who finally replies after three days.

That post that gets 12 likes instead of 2.

That video that makes you laugh so hard you wake up your partner.

Those rare hits are what keep the lever moving.

I've stayed up way past sensible hours waiting for one more "haha" reaction that never came.

The algorithm knows exactly how little reward it can give me before I give up — and it doles it out with surgical precision.

These five tricks — variable rewards, infinite scroll, social proof/FOMO, autoplay curation, intermittent reinforcement — aren't separate features.

They're a symphony.

Each one makes the others more powerful.

Together they create a machine that is better at capturing your attention than almost anything in human history.

The moment you see that and realize the tricks, the shame starts to lose its grip.

Which Distraction Avatar Are You Today?

Before we move on, we need a quick diagnostic. You can't fix a leak in the tank if you don't know where the hole is. Be honest—which of these "versions" of you took the wheel this morning?

The Tab Hoarder: You have 42 tabs open "just in case." You feel like closing one is deleting a piece of your future soul, even though three of them are recipes for sourdough you will never bake.

The Notification Junkie: You've developed a phantom vibration in your thigh. You check your phone not because you have a message, but because you're afraid you *don't*.

The Sudden-Idea Chaser: You start a client proposal and end up researching "How to start a goat farm in the Scenic Rim" because a thought crossed your mind and you "didn't want to forget it."

The Comparison Vampire: You were having a perfectly fine Wednesday until you saw a 22-year-old "lifestyle influencer" posting from a yacht. Now your air-conditioned office feels like a prison cell.

The First Quiet Rebellion

Here is the good news: The fact that you're even reading this—that you're aware enough to feel the tug of the hook—means your awareness is already higher than 90% of the population. You aren't losing; you've just been playing a game on "Expert Mode" without the rulebook.

We are not going to spend the rest of this book pretending you can throw your smartphone into the river and go live in a cave with a typewriter. You have a business to run. You have clients to answer. You have a life that requires you to be reachable.

But we *are* going to start a rebellion.

It's not a loud, flashy rebellion with banners and shouting. It's a quiet, sneaky one. We're going to start exploiting the rules of the casino. We're going to make your attention slightly less profitable to those Silicon Valley CEOs and tech companies and slightly more profitable to *you*.

We're going to stop fighting the system with willpower (which is a finite resource that usually runs out by 3:00 p.m. anyway) and start using systems that make focus the path of least resistance.

So, let's stop playing their game. Let's start playing ours.

In the next chapter, we're going to look at the "Twelve-Minute Brain"—how to build a wall around your focus that even the cleverest algorithm can't climb.

Ready? Put the phone face down. (Seriously. Do it now.)

Chapter 2: The Twelve-Minute Brain: Why You Can't Remember What You Started

The Lopsided Superhero (and the Science of Plasticity)

If you walked into a gym every day for three years and only ever did bicep curls with your right arm, you wouldn't be surprised when you eventually started looking like a lopsided superhero. You wouldn't blame your genetics, and you wouldn't go to the doctor complaining that your left arm was "broken." You'd intuitively understand that your body had simply adapted—with terrifying efficiency—to the specific, repetitive stress you put on it.

Your brain is no different.

Except instead of bicep curls, you've spent the last decade doing **Dopamine Sprints.**

We used to think the adult brain was like a piece of cured concrete—hard, set, and impossible to reshape after twenty-five. But modern neuroscience has given us a much more exciting (and slightly convicting) truth: **Neuroplasticity.** Your brain is more like high-grade silicone or a living map that is constantly being redrawn. Every time you perform an action, a cluster of neurons fires together. The more often they fire, the stronger the connection becomes. In the world of neuroscience, we call this Hebb's Law: *"Neurons that fire together, wire together."*

The "Pruning" Problem

Here's where the science gets a bit "Lawyer-like" in its cold efficiency. Your brain is a massive energy hog. It consumes about 20% of your body's calories despite being only 2% of your weight. To save energy, it practices something called **Synaptic Pruning**.

If you don't use a neural pathway, your brain assumes you don't need it anymore. It "prunes" the connection to save power, like a gardener cutting back dead branches to help the rest of the tree thrive.

When was the last time you sat for two hours and did nothing but read a complex legal brief or map out a sales strategy without checking a single notification? If the answer is *"I can't remember,"* then your "Deep Focus" highways have likely been pruned back to dirt tracks.

Meanwhile, that "Check the Phone" pathway? That thing is a ten-lane, illuminated super-highway.

The White Matter Shift

It's not just "mental habit"—it's physical structure. Research into heavy media multitaskers (people like us who have 14 tabs open and a phone in our hand) has shown a physical difference in the Anterior Cingulate Cortex (ACC)—the part of the brain responsible for emotional regulation and cognitive control.

A study from the University of Sussex found that people who frequently multitask across different media devices actually have lower grey-matter density in the ACC.

In plain English: We aren't just "distracted." We are physically thinning out the part of our brain that is supposed to be the "Brakes." We've spent so much time flooring the accelerator of novelty that we've let the brake pads wear down to the metal.

I see this in my own life constantly. I'll sit down at my desk in my home office, ready to be the "Managing Director" version of myself, but my brain is still in "Scrolling Mode." I'm trying to run a marathon on an arm that only knows how to do bicep curls.

The result? The **Twelve-Minute Itch.** Your brain has physically adapted to crave a new stimulus every few minutes. It's not a lack of willpower; it's a biological mandate. Your brain is just doing what you trained it to do.

The 12-Minute Itch (The Internal Interruption)

Imagine you've finally achieved the "Productivity Holy Grail." You are in a silent office, the door is locked, and your phone is switched off in a drawer. You sit down to tackle the big project—the one that requires real cognitive heavy lifting.

You're three minutes in. You're reading. You're thinking. And then, out of nowhere, a thought pops up: *"I wonder if I turned the dishwasher on?"* Or: *"I should probably check if that flight to Sydney has gone up in price."*

You didn't get a notification. No one knocked. You interrupted *yourself.*

The "Self-Interruption" Statistic

This isn't just a personal quirk; it's a documented biological rhythm. Research from the University of California, Irvine, found that we are responsible for about **half** of our own distractions. We interrupt ourselves almost as often as external forces do.

Why? Because your brain has become a **Dopamine Junkie**.

When you've spent years responding to external pings every few minutes, your brain develops a "clock." Around the 12-minute mark, your dopamine levels start to dip. Your brain, sensing the lack of "novelty," starts to panic. If an external distraction doesn't arrive to save the day, your brain will manufacture one from your own subconscious just to get that hit of "new information."

The "Urge to Check" is a Physical Itch

Think of it like a literal itch on your back. The more you try to ignore it, the more "urgent" it feels. In the attention economy, this is called **Intermittent Reinforcement**. Because you *sometimes* find something life-changing or hilarious when you check your brain's random impulses, the "Check" becomes a reinforced behavior.

I see this constantly in my direct sales business. I'll be halfway through a training module, and my brain will suddenly decide I desperately need to know the capital of Estonia.

Spoiler: Knowing the capital of Estonia (it's Tallinn, by the way) does not help me close a sale. But for those thirty seconds, my brain convinced me it was the most important information on the planet.

The "Zeigarnik Effect" Gone Wrong

We are also fighting a psychological phenomenon called the **Zeigarnik Effect**, as previously mentioned. This too plays a role in that "itch."

This is where the "Busy Professional" persona usually takes a hit. We love to brag about multitasking—it's the ultimate corporate flex. But as we're about to see, your brain isn't actually a parallel processor; it's a series of toggles that are wearing out.

The Myth of Multitasking (The "Switching Cost")

If I asked you to walk and chew gum at the same time, you'd do it perfectly. That's because walking is a motor function handled by the cerebellum, and chewing is a rhythmic task that doesn't require "executive" thought. But if I asked you to write a complex legal contract while simultaneously listening to a podcast about the history of the Roman Empire, you would fail.

Miserably.

That's because both of those tasks require the **Prefrontal Cortex**—the CEO of your brain. And the CEO of your brain doesn't do "simultaneous." It does "sequential."

When you think you are multitasking, what you are actually doing is **Context Switching** (or "Rapid Toggling"). You are slamming your brain's focus from Task A to Task B and back again at high speeds.

The Cognitive Tax (and the 40% Penalty)

Every time you toggle, you pay a tax. Researchers at the University of Michigan and the American Psychological Association found that even brief mental blocks created by shifting between tasks can cost as much as **40% of someone's productive time.**

Imagine you're a lawyer billing $400 an hour. If you spent that hour "multitasking" between a brief, your emails, and a LinkedIn thread, you didn't actually provide $400 worth of value. You provided $240, and you set $160 on fire just by switching tabs.

Why? Because of **Attention Residue.**

Coined by Dr. Sophie Leroy (sound familiar Book 1 readers?), this concept explains that when you switch from Task A to Task B, your attention doesn't follow you immediately. A "residue" of your thoughts stays stuck on the previous task. If you were just looking at a heated email from a client, and then you open a spreadsheet to do your

BAS, 20% of your brain is still drafting a snarky reply to that client.

You are effectively working with a "fragmented" brain. You're trying to solve a high-level problem with only three-quarters of your processing power available.

The "Rapid Toggling" Fatigue

This is why you feel exhausted at 5:00 p.m. even if you didn't actually *finish* anything.

Toggling requires an immense amount of metabolic energy. Every time you switch focus, your brain has to:

1. **Detach** from the current rules and goals.
2. **Locate** the rules and goals for the new task.
3. **Engage** with the new context.

Doing this fifty times an hour is the mental equivalent of doing fifty sprints in the midday sun. You aren't "busy"; you're just running in circles and wondering why you're out of breath.

I once spent an entire morning "multitasking" a sales strategy while "keeping an eye" on a team chat. By lunch, I had three half-finished ideas, a headache, and the sudden urge to take a nap under my desk. I hadn't done the work; I had just worn out my "toggling" muscle.

The goal for the rest of this book isn't to make you "faster" at multitasking. It's to stop the toggling entirely so you can actually use 100% of the brain you're paying for.

The Dopamine Debt Collector – Why You Feel Exhausted Even When You "Did Nothing"

Let's try and use another analogy and examples. We really need to knuckle this down. You've spent the day "working" — toggling, checking, replying, scrolling, thinking about replying, thinking about scrolling — and by 5 p.m. you're shattered. Your body feels like it ran a half-marathon, but your to-do list looks like it's been through a paper shredder backwards. Welcome to the Dopamine Debt Collector.

Every time you chase a quick hit (notification, tab switch, "brilliant" mid-task idea), your brain releases a micro-dose of dopamine — the chemical that says *"yes, good, more of that."* It's a tiny loan with very high interest. The more loans you take out during the day, the bigger the bill at sunset. And unlike a bank, the Debt Collector doesn't send polite reminders. It just shows up at 5 p.m. wearing steel-capped boots and says: *"Pay up, mate."*

You feel foggy, irritable, hungry for sugar or caffeine, and weirdly empty — even though you've been "busy" all day. That's not laziness. That's withdrawal. Your brain has been mainlining micro-hits of novelty so consistently that normal, slow-burn satisfaction (the kind you get from finishing a hard task) now feels flat. It's like eating fairy floss for lunch every day — by dinner, real food tastes like cardboard.

I've lived this cycle more times than I'd like to admit. I'd finish a day of "productive" toggling — Slack, email, LinkedIn, a quick scroll to "reset," another quick scroll to "celebrate," a third scroll because the first two weren't enough — and collapse on the couch feeling like I'd been hit by a bus that never arrived. My partner would ask *"How was your day?"* and I'd genuinely answer *"I have no idea... I think I did stuff?"* The Debt Collector had already taken his cut: mental clarity, emotional bandwidth, and the quiet pride of actually finishing something.

The brutal-but-liberating truth: You're not exhausted because you worked too hard. You're exhausted because you borrowed too much cheap dopamine and now the interest is due.

The Focus Debt Ceiling – How to Spot When You're About to Bounce the Cheque

Here's where we stop being victims and start being accountants — at least for a minute. Your brain has a rough daily limit on how many cheap-dopamine loans it can service before the whole system starts to wobble. Call it the Focus Debt Ceiling. Most of us hit it somewhere between 40–80 micro-interruptions a day (pings, self-interruptions, tab switches, "quick checks"). Past that point, the Debt Collector doesn't just knock — he kicks the door in.

Early warning signs you're approaching the ceiling:

- You re-read the same sentence four times and still don't know what it says
- You feel a vague, restless itch behind your eyes
- You start fantasizing about reorganizing your desk instead of doing the task
- You open your email just to feel "in control," then close it without replying to anything
- You get irrationally annoyed at perfectly normal things (the kettle taking too long, the font on your screen looking "wrong")

I call these "pre-bounce symptoms." They're not moral failings. They're your prefrontal cortex waving a tiny white flag: "*We're overdrawn. Can we stop spending please?*"

The good news: once you learn to spot the ceiling coming, you can decide whether to keep borrowing (and pay the price later) or declare a mini-bankruptcy right then and there — close tabs, step away, forgive the debt, and start fresh with what's left in the tank.

I've started treating those moments like a smoke alarm. When I feel the itch behind my eyes and catch myself thinking "maybe I should research the best noise-cancelling headphones again," I don't fight it. I just say out loud (yes, out loud — it helps): "*Debt Collector's at the door. Time to close the account for today.*" Then I shut the laptop, walk to the kitchen, make a fresh coffee, and stare out the window for three minutes like a confused philosopher. It's not elegant. But it's cheaper than letting the Collector repossess my entire evening.

From Debt to Surplus – The Quiet Promise of the Rest of This Book

Here's the hopeful bit we've been circling toward: Your brain can get out of debt. Not overnight. Not by willpower alone. But by changing the spending habits — one less loan, one longer stretch between hits, one afternoon where you let the slow, unsexy work actually finish.

Neuroplasticity cuts both ways. The same pruning and rewiring that turned your deep-focus highways into dirt tracks can rebuild them — if you give them consistent traffic instead of letting them grow over.

We're not going to pretend the rest of this book turns you into a laser-focused robot who never checks their phone again. That's not realistic, and frankly it sounds exhausting. What we're going to do is give you small, sneaky, forgiving ways to:

- Lower the interest rate on the dopamine you do borrow
- Spot the Debt Collector before he kicks the door in
- Build tiny stretches of surplus focus that feel good enough to repeat
- Forgive yourself when you overdraw anyway (because you will)

You're not starting from zero. You already know how to start (even if it's messy). Now we're going to teach you how to stay — not perfectly, not forever, but longer than twelve minutes at a time.

Because the opposite of debt isn't austerity. It's surplus. A little bit of mental breathing room. A quiet sense that you spent the afternoon on something that matters instead of something that just felt urgent.

That's what the rest of these pages are for. No magic. No monk-mode. Just slightly better afternoons, one forgiven overdraw at a time.

So if you're sitting there right now feeling the familiar itch behind your eyes — welcome. You're not broken. You're just overdrawn. And the bank is open for renegotiation.

Let's go see how much surplus we can claw back.

Chapter 3: The "Mute Everything Except Oxygen" Experiment

It's 9:48 a.m. on a Tuesday that has already threatened to be average. You've done the heroic thing: you've sat down, coffee in hand, laptop open, cursor blinking like it's daring you to type something meaningful. You've even managed to ignore the siren call of the dishwasher for once. You're in the chair. You're ready. You start typing the first sentence of whatever beast you're supposed to tame today — a proposal, a strategy doc, the opening paragraph of the thing you've been promising yourself since last summer.

And then the first notification lands. Not loud. Not angry. Just… polite. A soft chime. A tiny red dot. A whisper from the ether: "*Hey… someone liked your story from last Thursday when you tried to look thoughtful in natural light.*" You glance. You tell yourself: "*One second. I'll just dismiss it.*" You swipe. You mute that app. Then another app chimes. You mute that one too. Six minutes later you're deep in the settings menu, turning off badges, disabling banners, wondering why your phone has seventeen different ways to say "look at me" and why you feel personally attacked by every single one.

You haven't written another word. You've become the world's most dedicated notification bouncer. And the proposal is still sitting there with one lonely sentence staring back at you like a disappointed parent.

I've lived this exact loop more mornings than I care to count. I once spent a full twenty-three minutes "preparing my environment" by muting, silencing, do-not-disturb-ing every possible thing… only to open my email "just to make sure nothing urgent came in" and lose the next forty-seven minutes to a thread about whether oat milk is a war crime. By the time I looked up, my coffee was cold, my focus was gone, and I'd successfully muted everything except my own brain's ability to sabotage itself.

That's when I realized: Muting isn't the problem. Muting **while trying to work** is the problem. It's like trying to meditate in the middle of a construction site while wearing noise-cancelling headphones — you're still spending all your energy managing the noise instead of actually getting quiet.

So, I tried something stupidly simple. I called it the "Mute Everything Except Oxygen" experiment. The rule was brutal in its simplicity: For one fixed block of time (start small — 45 minutes is plenty), mute **literally everything** that isn't required for basic human survival. No exceptions for Slack. No exceptions for email previews. No exceptions for that one friend who "might text something important." If it doesn't keep your lungs working or stop your house from burning down, it gets muted.

No new apps. No complicated routines. No monk vows. Just silence — the kind you can actually afford without moving to a cave.

The first time I tried it, I lasted nineteen minutes. Nineteen glorious, itchy, uncomfortable minutes. My brain screamed like a toddler denied screen time: *"But what if someone needs you? What if there's news? What if you miss the meme that finally explains your entire personality?"* I sat there sweating through the panic, hands hovering over the phone like it was a live grenade. Then something weird happened. Around minute twenty, the screaming quietened. Not gone — just… quieter. I looked at the document again. I typed another sentence. Then another. By minute thirty-seven I'd written more than I had in the previous three mornings combined.

It wasn't magic. It wasn't enlightenment. It was just… fewer things shouting at me. For once, my own thoughts got to finish a sentence.

That's all this experiment is. A deliberately boring, low-stakes, reversible way to turn down the volume so your brain gets a turn to speak — without making you feel like you're punishing yourself or joining a cult that hates fun.

You don't have to do it forever. You don't have to do it perfectly. You just have to do it once — long enough to notice what happens when the noise floor drops and the only thing left talking is you.

Most people discover one of three things:

1. The world keeps turning even when you're not instantly reachable.

2. Your brain panics at first because it's used to constant stimulation — but the panic passes faster than you expect.

3. When the noise drops, the work doesn't magically become easy… but it does become possible.

And possible is all we're asking for right now.

So, here's the invitation: Pick one block tomorrow — 45 minutes is plenty. Mute everything except oxygen (and maybe calls from actual humans if you want to be practical). Set a timer. Sit with the discomfort. Watch what your brain does when it's not being constantly interrupted by tiny dopamine sprinkles.

No judgment if you cave at seventeen minutes. No gold star if you last the full forty-five. Just curiosity.

Because the first rebellion isn't about winning the war against distraction. It's about giving yourself sixty seconds of quiet so you can hear what you actually want to say — instead of what the slot machine wants you to hear.

Ready to try turning down the volume? Let's see what happens when the only thing left screaming is your own thoughts.

(And yes — if they scream "check your phone" for the first twelve minutes, that's normal. We'll talk about why in a second.)

Why Volume Matters More Than You Think

Let's be brutally honest for a second: most of us don't realize how loud our days actually are until we turn the volume down — even a little. We think the problem is "*I don't have enough time*" or "*I'm not motivated enough.*" But half the time the real problem is simpler and sneakier: There's so much background noise that our own thoughts can't get a word in edgewise.

Think of your attention like a small apartment in the middle of a busy Sydney street. There's traffic outside (notifications, Slack pings, email banners). There's construction next door (autoplay videos, infinite feeds).

There's a neighbor with a leaf blower (your own brain inventing emergencies every twelve minutes). And you're trying to have a quiet conversation with yourself about the thing that actually matters — that proposal, that strategy, that one paragraph you've been avoiding for weeks.

Now imagine someone finally turns off the leaf blower, the traffic thins out, and the construction crew takes their smoke break. Suddenly you can hear yourself think. Not perfectly. Not in silence like a mountain retreat. Just… clearer. The words come a little easier. The itch behind your eyes backs off for a bit. You don't become a productivity robot — you just become a person who can finish a sentence without nineteen side quests.

That's what lowering the volume does. It doesn't eliminate distraction forever (good luck with that in 2026). It creates tiny pockets of surplus attention — little surpluses of mental breathing room — so your brain can actually spend its energy on the work instead of on managing the chaos.

Here's why the noise matters more than most productivity advice admits:

1. **Constant low-level pings keep your nervous system on simmer** Every chime, every red dot, every banner is a micro-adrenaline hit. Your sympathetic nervous system (the fight-or-flight one) never fully stands down. It's like having a smoke alarm that beeps every three minutes — not loud enough to evacuate the building, but loud enough that you never really relax. Over hours, that low simmer burns through your Decision Tokens faster than you realize. By 2 p.m. you're not just tired — you're physiologically primed to chase the next quick hit because your body thinks it's still in mild danger.

2. **Background hum crowds out deep work** Deep focus isn't just about willpower. It needs cognitive bandwidth — the mental equivalent of RAM. Every open tab, every pending notification, every "I should probably check that later" thought is taking up a tiny slice of that RAM. Even if you're not actively looking at them, your brain is running background scans: "Don't forget me. Don't forget me." By mid-morning, you're trying to write a

complex argument with only 60% of your processing power available. No wonder it feels like wading through mud.

3. **Noise trains your brain to expect constant input** Remember neuroplasticity from Chapter 2? The pathways you use the most get stronger; the ones you ignore get pruned. If your brain spends most of its day fielding interruptions, it gets very good at fielding interruptions — and very bad at ignoring them. Silence starts to feel wrong. Boredom starts to feel dangerous. That's why, when you finally mute everything, the first ten minutes often feel like torture — your brain is literally withdrawing from the noise it's been trained to crave.

But here's the hopeful flip side: Lowering the volume even a little retrains those pathways in the other direction. Not overnight. Not perfectly. But enough that, after a few experiments, forty-five minutes of quiet stops feeling like punishment and starts feeling like… relief. Like breathing after being underwater too long.

I'm not promising you'll become one of those terrifying people who *"only check their phone twice a day."* I'm promising you'll get a few extra pockets of time where your own thoughts get to finish what they started — and that feels surprisingly good.

So, when you try the "Mute Everything Except Oxygen" block tomorrow and the itch hits at minute twelve, remember: That itch isn't proof you're failing. It's proof your brain has been living in a very loud apartment for a long time. It's just not used to quiet yet. Give it a few more minutes. It might surprise you.

The rest of this chapter (and the book) is about making those quiet pockets easier to find and longer to stay in — without turning your life into a monastery or pretending you never want to scroll again.

Because the goal isn't to hate your phone. It's to stop letting the phone hate your afternoons.

The Experiment Rules – Keep It Stupidly Simple

Now that we've established why the noise is quietly murdering your afternoons, let's make the fix as embarrassingly easy as possible. No new apps you'll have to learn. No life-coach vows you'll break by Wednesday.

No "digital minimalism" manifesto that makes you feel like you're betraying your entire personality.

The "Mute Everything Except Oxygen" experiment is deliberately boring. That's the point. Boring works when flashy fails.

Here are the stupidly simple rules. You can read them once, do them tomorrow morning, and never think about them again until you want to.

Rule 1: Pick a tiny, realistic block Start with 45 minutes. Not two hours. Not "the whole afternoon." 45 minutes is long enough to feel like you've done something, short enough that your brain won't stage a full mutiny. If 45 feels too ambitious, drop to 30. If you're feeling heroic, stretch to 60 or 90. But 45 is the sweet spot — it's roughly one Pomodoro plus coffee time, minus the smugness.

Rule 2: Mute literally everything that isn't breathing-related

- Phone → Do Not Disturb on. Exceptions: only actual phone calls from people in your "favorites" list (mum, partner, best mate, whoever would actually show up if your house was on fire). No texts, no app alerts, no WhatsApp, no Slack previews.

- Email client → Close the tab or app completely. If you must keep it open for "emergencies," turn off all sounds, banners, and badge counts. The red dot is a tiny guilt bomb — defuse it.
- Browser → Turn off all website notifications (Chrome/Edge/Safari settings — one click in the address bar for most sites). Close every tab that isn't the one you're working on. Yes, all of them.
- Slack/Teams/whatever chat app → Set status to "Offline" or "Do Not Disturb." If your workplace culture will implode without you, mute channels instead of the whole app — but be ruthless.
- Music/podcasts → If you use background sound, pick one thing and let it play. No switching playlists mid-block. No "just finding the perfect lo-fi beats station." One station. Press play. Done.

Rule 3: Set a real timer (not your phone) Use the microwave, the oven timer, a cheap kitchen egg timer, the stopwatch on your ancient sports watch — anything that ticks audibly and can't be silently dismissed with a thumb.

Why not the phone? Because the phone is the problem. If you use the phone timer, you'll "just check one thing" while setting it. Trust me. I've lived this.

Rule 4: When the itch hits — name it, don't fight it Around minute 12–18, your brain will throw a tantrum. It will invent emergencies: *"Did I lock the car?" "Is the cat judging me?" "I should probably check if that flight to Melbourne is cheaper now."* When it happens, don't argue. Just say out loud (yes, out loud — it's weirdly powerful): *"Ah, there's the Debt Collector knocking again."* Or: *"Nice try, brain. That's a shiny-object invoice — I'll pay it at 5 p.m."* Naming it without judgment takes away half its power. You're not failing. You're observing. Big difference.

Rule 5: When the timer beeps — stop No *"just one more sentence."* No *"I was almost in flow."* Beep = done. Stand up. Stretch. Drink water. Look out the window like a confused philosopher for sixty seconds. Then decide: do you want to run another block, or call it a win and move on?

That's it. No complicated scoring system. No app to track your "streak." No guilt if you only last nineteen minutes the first time. You're not training for the focus

Olympics. You're just giving your brain a short holiday from the construction site.

Most people who try this for the first time report one of three outcomes:

- They last the full block and feel weirdly proud — like they just survived a mild natural disaster.
- They cave at 18–25 minutes, feel a bit defeated… then realize they still got more done in those 18 minutes than in the previous two hours of "multitasking."
- They discover their own thoughts are louder (and sometimes weirder) than the notifications — and that's both uncomfortable and oddly refreshing.

All three are wins. Because the goal isn't perfection. It's data. And data beats shame every single time.

So tomorrow morning — or whenever your next realistic 45-minute window appears — give it a go. Mute everything except oxygen. Set the timer. Sit with the itch. See what happens when the noise drops and the only thing left talking is you.

No pressure. No judgment. Just one quiet experiment.

And if your brain spends the whole block trying to convince you that reorganising your Spotify playlists is suddenly urgent… well, at least you'll know exactly who's been running the show all this time.

Making It Stick Without Hating Yourself

So you've tried the experiment. Maybe you lasted 19 minutes and felt like a fraud. Maybe you hit the full 45 and felt like you'd just pulled off a small bank heist against your own wiring. Either way — congratulations. You've done something most people never do: you turned the volume down on purpose for a bit. That alone is a win. Now the question is: how do you keep doing it without it feeling like punishment, without it turning into another "should" that you eventually rebel against, and without losing the sense of humour that got you this far?

The short answer: make it stupidly easy, stupidly forgiving, and stupidly rewarding. Here are the ways I (and plenty of other recovering scroll zombies) have managed to turn a 45-minute mute block into something that happens more days than not — without ever feeling like I'm living in a monastery or betraying my inner chaos goblin.

1. Shrink the ask until it's laughably small If 45 minutes still feels like climbing Everest in thongs, drop it to 20. Or 15. Or — on really rough mornings — 10. The goal isn't duration at first; it's repetition. Ten minutes of quiet every day for a week beats one heroic 90-minute session followed by three days of avoidance. I started with 12-minute blocks because 12 minutes felt like nothing — literally the length of one average YouTube video. If I could survive 12 minutes without checking my phone, I could survive anything. And once 12 became normal, 20 felt easy. Then 30. Then 45. The secret isn't willpower. It's starting so small that your brain can't justify a rebellion.

2. Pair it with something you already love (temptation bundling, but make it lazy) Tie the mute block to a ritual you don't hate. After you make your morning coffee → mute everything and write for 20 minutes while the coffee cools. After you finish breakfast → mute and tackle the first hard thing while your stomach settles. After you walk the dog → mute and do one focused block before the day explodes. The brain loves patterns. If "coffee = quiet" becomes the association, you'll start craving the quiet because it comes with caffeine and no guilt. I now associate the smell of fresh coffee with "phone goes in the drawer." It's Pavlovian. And it works better than any motivational poster ever could.

3. Build in a guilt-free escape hatch When the itch hits and you're tempted to cave, give yourself permission to bail — but with one tiny condition: name the reason out loud. *"I'm caving because my brain wants dopamine." "I'm caving because I'm bored and scared of what I'll find if I keep writing." "I'm caving because the neighbor's renovating again and it sounds like a demolition derby."* Naming it strips the shame. You're not failing — you're collecting data. And data beats self-loathing every time. Most people find that once they name the urge, they often keep going anyway. The urge loses power when it's not allowed to hide.

4. Reward the effort, not the outcome After the block — win or cave — give yourself something small and immediate that feels good:

- A fresh coffee.
- Five minutes of guilt-free scrolling (yes, really — set a timer).
- A quick walk around the block.

- A funny meme you've been saving. The reward isn't for "being perfect." It's for showing up and trying. Your brain learns: "Quiet time = good things happen after." That's how habits stick — not through discipline, but through tiny bribes and zero judgment.

5. Track it with the world's laziest system No fancy app. No streak tracker that will guilt you into oblivion. Just a Post-it note on your desk or a note in your phone called "Mute Experiments." After each block, write one line: "20 min. Caved at 14. Brain wanted to Google 'best noise-cancelling headphones again.' Laughed. Next time 22." That's it. No scores. No percentages. Just a little log that shows you're moving — even when it feels like you're not.

The beauty of this approach is that it doesn't ask you to become someone else. It asks you to stay exactly who you are — messy, curious, prone to distraction, in love with coffee and memes — and just give yourself a few more minutes of quiet every day.

Because the opposite of constant noise isn't silence forever. It's enough quiet to hear yourself finish a thought.

And once you hear that thought finish… you might actually like what it has to say.

So tomorrow — or the next day that doesn't feel like total chaos — run the experiment again. Mute everything except oxygen. Set the timer. Name the itch when it arrives. Reward yourself after. Log one line.

No pressure. No perfection. Just one more quiet pocket in a loud world.

Chapter 4: The Physical Exile Rule (AKA Put the Damn Thing in Another Room)

Why Proximity Is the Real Enemy

Here's the uncomfortable truth nobody wants to admit: even when your phone is silent, face-down, on Do Not Disturb, and technically "not bothering you," it's still winning. It's still taking up space in your head. Not metaphorically — literally. Research keeps showing the same weird result: the **mere presence** of a phone (even turned off, even in another person's bag across the room) reduces working memory, problem-solving ability, and cognitive performance. It's called the "brain drain" effect. Your prefrontal cortex — the part that's supposed to be running the show — quietly allocates a tiny slice of its bandwidth to monitoring the device: "*Is it ringing? Is it vibrating? Did I miss something?*" Even if you consciously ignore it, part of you is still on guard duty.

Think of it like having a needy flatmate who's promised to be quiet for an hour. They're sitting in the corner, not saying a word. But you still feel watched. You still adjust your behaviour. You still can't fully relax into whatever you're doing because some ancient part of your brain is running a background scan: "Threat level? Still low? Still low? Okay, but check again in 30 seconds."

That's why muting helps — it turns down the volume — but it doesn't eliminate the presence. The phone is still there. Still visible. Still within arm's reach. And your brain knows it.

I learned this the hard way. I'd mute everything, put the phone face-down on the desk "just in case," and then spend the next 45 minutes hyper-aware of its existence. Every few minutes my eyes would flick over to it — not to check it, just to confirm it was still there. It was like having a sleeping toddler in the room: you're trying to work, but part of you is always listening for the first cry. I got less done with the phone muted on my desk than I did when I completely forgot about it.

The fix isn't complicated. It's drastic in the moment, but dead simple: Get the damn thing out of the room.

Not in a drawer. Not on another desk. Another **room**. Somewhere that requires you to stand up, walk, open a door, and close it behind you. The friction is the point. Every extra step makes the "just quick check" impulse cost more calories than it's worth.

Why does this work better than muting alone?

- It eliminates the mere-presence drain completely.
- It forces a physical interruption to any "I'll just peek" urge — by the time you've walked to the kitchen/laundry/bedroom, the urgency usually evaporates.
- It creates a clear boundary: "In here = work time. Out there = everything else."
- Your brain gets the signal that the slot machine is temporarily closed for business — and surprisingly often, it stops asking to play.

I once exiled my phone to the laundry basket during a 60-minute writing block. Halfway through, I convinced myself the washing machine was flooding (it wasn't). I walked in there, checked the phone (still silent), checked the machine (fine), walked back, and kept writing. I burned more energy on that ridiculous errand than I would have on twenty minutes of scrolling — and I finished the block with actual words on the page.

The exile isn't about hating your phone. It's about loving your own attention enough to give it a short holiday from the thing that's been renting space in your head rent-free for years.

So tomorrow — or the next time you have a realistic 30–60 minute window — try it. Pick your block. Pick an exile location (kitchen counter, bedroom dresser, top of the fridge — somewhere that feels like a different country). Say out loud (yes, out loud — it helps): "*You're going on holiday for 45 minutes. Don't cause international incidents.*" Walk it there. Close the door. Come back to your desk. Set a real timer. Sit down.

And see what happens when the needy flatmate isn't even in the building anymore.

Most people discover one of three things:

1. The world keeps turning without their constant supervision.

2. Their brain panics at first ("What if someone needs me?") — but the panic fades faster than expected when there's no phone to check.

3. When the presence is gone, the work doesn't become magically easy… but it does become possible. And possible is all we're chasing right now.

No judgment if you fetch it at 22 minutes because you "forgot" you were doing an experiment. No gold star if you last the full hour. Just curiosity.

Because the first real freedom isn't never touching the phone again. It's realizing you can leave it in another room for 45 minutes and still be okay — maybe even better than okay.

And when you walk back in to retrieve it and see that zero emergencies happened… well, that's when the quiet starts to feel less like punishment and more like a gift you gave yourself.

Ready to send your phone on a very short, very local holiday? Let's see what happens when the needy flatmate isn't even in the postcode.

The Physical Exile Rules – Make It Ridiculously Easy

Right — we've established that having the phone in the same postcode as your work is like trying to concentrate while a needy toddler keeps poking you in the ribs going "hey… hey… hey…" Muting helps, but proximity still drains you. So the fix is brutally straightforward: Get it out of the room. Not "out of sight." Out of **room**.

Here are the rules so stupidly simple that even I — a person who once forgot where I exiled my own phone and spent 15 minutes retracing my steps like a confused detective — can follow them.

Rule 1: Pick your block length (keep it embarrassingly short at first) Start with 30 minutes. That's it. 30 minutes is long enough to feel like you've done something meaningful, short enough that your brain can't mount a full-scale rebellion. If 30 feels like a stretch, drop to 20. If you're feeling briefly heroic, go 45. But 30 is the Goldilocks zone — not too scary, not too pointless.

Rule 2: Choose an exile destination that requires actual walking Not the other side of your desk. Not the drawer next to you. Another **room**. Kitchen counter. Bedroom dresser. Laundry basket (bonus points if it's on top of yesterday's clothes). Top of the fridge (my personal favorite — it feels like sending the phone to timeout in the naughty corner). The point is friction: you have to stand up, walk, open a door, and close it behind you. Every extra step makes the "just quick peek" impulse cost more effort than it's worth. I once chose the laundry because it's at the opposite end of the flat — by the time I'd walked there and back I'd already burned more calories than I would have scrolling.

Rule 3: Do the exile ritual (yes, make it a tiny ceremony — it helps)

1. Pick your block duration and say it out loud: "Thirty minutes. Phone, you're going on a very short holiday." (Speaking it aloud is cheesy but weirdly powerful — it tricks your brain into treating it like a real commitment.)
2. Physically pick up the phone.
3. Walk it to the exile spot.

4. Put it down face-down (or screen-off if you're paranoid).

5. Say (again, out loud if you're alone): "Behave. No international incidents while I'm gone."

6. Close the door if there is one.

7. Walk back to your desk.

8. Set a real, physical timer in the room you're working in (microwave, egg timer, oven — anything that isn't the phone). That's it. Eight steps. Takes 45 seconds. Most of the resistance dies in those 45 seconds.

Rule 4: When the itch hits — name it and let it expire Around minute 10–15, your brain will start inventing reasons to go fetch it: "Did I leave it on silent or vibrate?" "What if someone needs me right now?" "I should check if the washing machine is flooding." (Yes, I've invented washing-machine emergencies mid-block.) Don't argue. Don't fight. Just name it silently or out loud. The urge often passes in under a minute once it's not allowed to hide.

Rule 5: When the timer beeps — retrieve it guilt-free No "just one more sentence." Beep = done. Stand up.

Walk to the exile spot. Pick up the phone. Unlock it if you want. Check whatever you need to check. The world will still be there. And nine times out of ten, exactly zero emergencies happened while you were gone. That realization — "I was unreachable for 30 minutes and nothing collapsed" — is quietly addictive. It's the opposite of FOMO. It's FOGO: Fear Of Getting Organized. You start craving those little pockets of "nothing happened" because they feel like freedom.

This isn't about hating your phone. It's about loving your own attention enough to give it a short, drama-free holiday from the thing that's been renting space in your head rent-free for years.

What Actually Happens When You Exile It (And Why It's Weirdly Liberating)

You've done the ritual. Phone is in the laundry basket / on top of the fridge / in the spare bedroom with the door closed like it's been sent to its room for bad behavior. You're back at your desk. Timer is ticking. The room feels… empty. Not silent — just… less crowded. And then the comedy begins.

Minute 0–10: The Phantom Limb Phase Your brain hasn't quite accepted the exile. You keep reaching for the spot where the phone usually lives — like a missing limb you still feel itching. You glance at the empty desk corner every 90 seconds. You think: "What if someone's trying to reach me right now? What if there's a fire? What if the cat's stuck somewhere?" None of these thoughts are rational. They're just phantom vibrations from a lifetime of conditioning. I've caught myself patting my empty pocket like I'm checking for a wallet I haven't carried in years. It's ridiculous. And it passes.

Minute 10–20: The Panic Spike This is the make-or-break window. The brain realizes the slot machine is literally in another postcode and starts negotiating: "*Okay, but can we just go look at it? Just to make sure it's still alive?*" "*I promise I won't unlock it. I just want to see the screen is off.*" "I think I left it on silent — what if it's vibrating and I can't hear it?" You feel restless. Your leg bounces. Your eyes dart to the hallway like you're expecting a rescue team to burst in and say "*You forgot your phone!*" This is the Debt Collector's last desperate attempt to collect early. Most people cave here the first time. That's fine. You still lasted longer than if the phone had been sitting next to you. The ones who push through usually do it by naming the urge out loud: *"Ah, there's the panic spike. Classic."* Or: *"Brain, you're adorable when you're dramatic."* Naming it turns the panic into a punchline. And punchlines are easier to sit with than panic.

Minute 20–40: The Quiet Settles In Something shifts. The urgency fades. The room stops feeling empty and starts feeling… spacious. Your thoughts slow down — not in a bad way, just in a "oh, I can actually finish this sentence" way. You type a paragraph. You re-read it. It doesn't suck. You type another one. The work isn't suddenly easy — it's still work — but it's work without nineteen competing radio stations playing in the background. You notice things: The way your coffee smells when it's cooling. The faint sound of traffic outside. The fact that your own thoughts have volume when nothing else is shouting. It's not enlightenment. It's just… room. Mental elbow room. And elbow room feels surprisingly good after years of mental overcrowding.

Minute 40+: The Quiet Surprise (and the Walk-Back Test) The timer beeps. You stand up. You walk to the exile spot. You pick up the phone. You look at it. No missed calls. No urgent texts. No world-ending notifications. Exactly zero emergencies happened while you were gone. And that realization hits like a gentle slap: *"I was unreachable for 40 minutes… and nothing collapsed."* It's not dramatic. It's not life-changing in a fireworks way. It's just… quiet proof that the world can spin without your constant supervision. And that proof is addictive in the best way. You start craving those little "nothing happened" pockets because they feel like freedom instead of deprivation.

I've had blocks where I wrote more in 35 minutes than in the previous three days combined. I've had blocks where I only managed one decent paragraph — but it was a paragraph that existed because I stayed in the room instead of fleeing to the next dopamine hit. Both count as wins. Because the metric isn't perfection. It's presence.

The hilarious part? The more you exile the phone, the less dramatic the panic becomes. The first few times feel like separation anxiety. By the fifth or sixth, it's more like *"yeah, yeah, I'll go check on it in a minute — it's fine."* Your brain learns: "Phone in another room = nothing bad happens." And once it learns that, the exile stops feeling like punishment and starts feeling like… a favor you're doing for yourself.

So when you run the exile tomorrow and your brain throws every excuse it can invent — from "the washing machine is flooding" to "I think I left the stove on" — don't fight it. Don't judge it. Just watch it like you're at the cinema watching a very over-acted comedy. Because that's what it is: Your brain doing its best impression of a toddler who's just discovered sugar and the word "why."

The exile isn't the goal. The exile is the space where you finally get to be in the room with your own thoughts — without the needy flatmate hovering in the corner.

And when you walk back in to retrieve it and see that zero emergencies happened… well, that's when the quiet starts to feel less like a chore and more like a gift you gave yourself.

And that's it for exile. No grand finale. No fireworks. No life-altering epiphany where the clouds part and a choir sings.

Just this: Every time you walk the phone to another room and close the door behind it, you're quietly saying to yourself — and to the attention economy — "I'm worth a few minutes of my own company."

You're not becoming someone new. You're not winning the war. You're just taking back a little piece of your afternoon, one short holiday at a time.

And on the days when the exile lasts only 12 minutes, or when you fetch the phone early because the magpies are having a full-on turf war on the balcony and you need moral support — that's okay too. You still showed up. You still tried. You still gave yourself the gift of a few extra minutes where nothing was demanding your attention except the thing you actually wanted to do.

That's not failure. That's grace. And grace, my friend, is the quietest rebellion of all.

So next time the itch hits, or the Debt Collector knocks, or your brain invents a sudden need to reorganise the spice rack… smile. Pick up the phone. Walk it to its little timeout spot. Close the door. Come back to your desk. And sit with yourself for a bit.

Because you deserve to be in the room with your own thoughts — even if they're messy, even if they're itchy, even if they're still figuring out what they want to say.

And when you walk back in later and see that the world kept spinning without you glued to the screen… you might just feel something small, warm, and surprisingly steady.

That feeling? That's yours. No algorithm can sell it. No notification can steal it. It's just you — showing up for you, one exile at a time.

Chapter 5: One-Screen Monogamy & The Ninety-Minute Fake Deadline

Why Toggling Is the Silent Thief (And Why You're Paying a Massive Tax Every Time You Think You're "Multitasking")

Let's start with the uncomfortable bit nobody wants to say out loud: Most of us aren't multitasking. We're just very expensive, very slow, very tired context-switchers who've convinced ourselves we're efficient.

You open the laptop with noble intentions. The proposal doc is front and center. You start typing. Then Slack pings. You glance — "just to see if it's urgent." (still doing this – but the more I repeat myself, the more I hope it sinks in- sorry!) You reply with three words. Then you think "while I'm here I'll quickly check email." You open Gmail. You see one unread from a client. You open it. You start drafting a reply. Then you remember you need a number from the spreadsheet. You open the spreadsheet. You copy the number. You paste it into the email. You hit send. You go back to the proposal. You re-read the last sentence you wrote. You realize you have no idea what you were trying to say. You start again. Slack pings again. And round and round we go.

By 11:30 a.m. you feel like you've been working hard for two hours. You've sent one email, added one number to a spreadsheet, and written half a paragraph that you'll probably delete later. You're exhausted. Your to-do list is laughing at you. And you have the vague, nagging feeling that you've been robbed — but you can't quite put your finger on who did it.

Here's who: Your own brain, every time it toggles.

Every single switch — from proposal to Slack to email to spreadsheet and back — costs you. Not metaphorically. Literally. Studies (yes, boring academic ones) have measured the tax:

- Average time to fully re-engage after a switch: 23 minutes (some say up to 40).

- Productivity loss per frequent switcher: 20–40% of total available cognitive horsepower.

- Daily mental energy wasted on toggling for heavy multitaskers: equivalent to 2–3 hours of focused work that simply evaporates.

You're not "getting more done." You're paying a massive tax for the illusion of progress. You're running three half-marathons at the same time instead of finishing one properly — and wondering why you're always out of breath and never crossing any finish lines.

I lived this cycle for years. I'd brag about how "busy" I was — eight apps open, Slack on, email on, browser with 17 tabs, music playing "to help focus." I felt like a productivity superhero. By 3 p.m. I was a zombie who'd achieved exactly three things:

1. Sent one email I probably should have rewritten.

2. Added two lines to a spreadsheet I still didn't understand.

3. Collected a headache that lasted until bedtime.

I wasn't inefficient. I was just paying a tax I didn't know existed. Every toggle was a tiny transaction fee — 23 minutes here, 15 minutes there — and by the end of the day I'd paid enough fees to buy a small island of actual finished work… but I never got the island. I just had receipts.

The attention economy loves that tax. Every switch is another opportunity for a ping, a banner, a "recommended for you," a "quick check." The more you toggle, the more chances they get to sneak in. You think you're being responsive and flexible. They think you're being deliciously profitable.

Here's the hopeful (and slightly embarrassing) truth: You don't need to become a single-tasking saint who never opens more than one window ever again. You just need to stop paying the tax on every single block. One screen. One thing. One short, realistic window where the only thing visible is the thing you actually want to finish.

When you do that, the cost drops dramatically. Attention residue fades faster. The work doesn't become magically easy — it's still work — but it becomes possible. Possible is all we're asking for right now.

I once tried one-screen monogamy on a proposal I'd been avoiding for three weeks. I closed everything except the document. Full-screen. No tabs. No Slack. No email previews. I set a 60-minute timer and committed: one thing only. First 15 minutes: itch, restlessness, brain inventing emergencies ("I should check if the cat is judging me from the windowsill"). Next 45 minutes: quiet settled. I finished the proposal — not perfectly, but finished. It was the first time in months I'd sent something without sixteen tabs open like a safety net.

That's the quiet power of monogamy: You don't have to do it all day. Just one block. Then another. Each block is a tiny vote for "I can stay with one thing long enough to finish it."

And when you do? You get back something the attention economy can't sell: A little pocket of your afternoon that actually belonged to you.

No fireworks. No enlightenment. Just one less toggle, one more finished sentence, one more day where you weren't running in circles wondering why you're out of breath.

That's the rebellion. One screen. One thing. One slightly less fragmented you.

Chapter 6: Thought Quarantine – The "Write It and Forget It" Notebook

The Mid-Flow Hijack (The "Why")

If you've been following the steps in this book, you've reached a milestone that usually feels like a miracle: You actually started. You cleared the desk, you set your Ninety-Minute Fake Deadline, you practiced "One-Screen Monogamy," and for the first time in three days, you are actually doing the "Big Rock" task. You are in flow. The engine is humming.

Then, at exactly 10:42 a.m., it happens.

Out of nowhere, your brain shouts: *"Wait! Is the LinkedIn banner we're using still that photo from 2019? We look twelve years old in that. We should change it. Right now. It'll only take three minutes."*

In Book 1, we talked about the **Parking Lot**. I called it the "bouncer at the door." Its job is to stop the "Future Shiny BS*" from getting into the room while you're trying to sit down. But the distraction that hits you at 10:42 a.m. didn't come from the hallway. It came from *inside the house.*

Now for those returning from Book 1 – you might ask, is the Thought Quarantine the same thing as the Parking Lot idea?

Great question — and no, Thought Quarantine is not the same as the Parking Lot from Book 1.

They're cousins, not twins. Both are ways to stop random shiny thoughts from derailing you, but they serve slightly different purposes and work in different moments of the distraction cycle. Here's the clear, no-BS breakdown so you can see exactly how they differ and why having both in the toolkit makes sense.

Quick Side-by-Side Comparison

Aspect	Parking Lot (Book 1)	Thought Quarantine (Book 2)
Main job	Catch "ooh, shiny object" ideas that pop up while you're trying to do your Three Things	Catch "wait, I should do/research/think about this RIGHT NOW" urges that try to hijack you after you've already started focusing

Aspect	Parking Lot (Book 1)	Thought Quarantine (Book 2)
When it happens	Usually **before** or **during** the early stage of starting a task (the distraction arrives before momentum)	Usually **after** you've begun — when you're finally in flow and the brain suddenly goes "but what about…?"
Emotional flavor	"I'm avoiding the hard thing by chasing novelty"	"I'm sabotaging my own progress because the current task got momentarily boring/uncomfortable"
Physical action	Write the idea in a notebook, close the book, keep working on the original task	Write the intrusive thought on a separate small card/post-it, physically move it to a "quarantine box" or sealed envelope on your desk, leave it there until a designated review time (e.g., end of day or Friday)
Psychological trick	Gives the brain the illusion that the idea is "saved forever" so it stops nagging	Creates literal **physical distance + time delay** so the urgency feels fake; most thoughts lose 80% of their sparkle once they're quarantined for 4–6 hours

Aspect	Parking Lot (Book 1)	Thought Quarantine (Book 2)
Best for	Shiny-object specialists / chronic researchers who get hijacked before they even begin	People who finally start… then self-sabotage mid-flow with "brilliant" mid-task ideas
Humorous tagline	"Write it down, close the book - it's immortal now."	"Quarantine the thought like it has a suspicious cough — no visitors until Friday."

Why both are needed (and not redundant)

- **Parking Lot** is the bouncer at the door: it stops most distractions from even getting into your work session.

- **Thought Quarantine** is the medic inside the room: it deals with the ones that sneak past the bouncer and try to interrupt you **while you're already working**.

In real life, you need both because:

- Some distractions hit before you start (classic Book 1 problem → Parking Lot wins).

- Some hit **after** you've tricked yourself into starting (classic Book 2 problem → Thought Quarantine wins).

Most people experience both patterns on the same day, so having two slightly different tools stops the "oh this doesn't work for me" frustration when one tool alone isn't enough.

Example from a "real" day (made-up but very relatable)

You sit down to write a client proposal (your Big Rock).

- 9:14 a.m.: Brain says "I wonder if I should rebrand my entire website first?" → **Parking Lot** catches it. You write it on the notebook page titled "Future Shiny Bullshit," close the book, keep writing the proposal.

- 10:42 a.m.: You're finally in flow… then brain says "Wait, is my LinkedIn banner still using that old photo? I should update it right now!" → **Thought Quarantine**. You scribble it on a bright pink post-it, fold it, drop it into the little "Quarantine Box" (an old tea tin on your desk), and tell yourself "You can visit it at 5 p.m. if you still care." By 5 p.m. you usually don't.

Same problem (intrusive idea), different timing → different tool.

This is the **Mid-Flow Hijack**, and it is fundamentally different from the "I don't want to start" procrastination we usually talk about.

The Bouncer vs. The Medic

In my world as a lawyer and business owner, I've realized that distractions have different "entry points."

- **The Parking Lot (Book 1)** is for the "Ooh, shiny!" ideas that hit you before you've gained momentum. It's the bouncer that says, "Not today, buddy," and keeps the door locked so you can actually sit down.

- **The Thought Quarantine (Book 2)** is the "medic inside the room." It is for the intrusive thoughts that wait until you are vulnerable—usually right when the work gets a little bit boring, a little bit technical, or a little bit uncomfortable.

When you're mid-flow, your brain is like a high-performance engine. When a "random" thought like 'I *wonder if I should rebrand the entire website?"* pops up, it's not just a thought; it's a self-sabotage mechanism. Your brain has hit a pocket of resistance in your actual work, and it is desperately offering you a "productive-feeling" escape route.

The Emotional Flavor of Sabotage

The reason the Parking Lot often fails here is that these mid-task thoughts feel "valid." They don't feel like scrolling TikTok; they feel like *work*. You tell yourself, *"I'm already at the computer, it'll just take a second."* But here is the "No-BS" truth: If you follow that thought, you break the seal. You exit the "Vortex-Free Zone" you worked so hard to create. You aren't just checking a banner; you are telling your brain that your focus is for sale to the highest (and loudest) bidder.

You can't just "ignore" the thought, either. If you try to push it down, it stays open in the back of your mind like a browser tab you can't close, draining your mental battery and making you "Fashionably Late" to your own deadline. To stay in the zone, you need a way to acknowledge the thought, strip it of its urgency, and put it in a "Golden Cage" where it can't hurt your progress.

You need to quarantine the thought like it has a suspicious cough. No visitors allowed until the work is done.

Essentially, the parking lot is to "park" those ideas later, and stop them from getting in, whereas the thought quarantine is for those that manage to actually sneak in persistently – so you quarantine them and keep the party going!

The Physical Quarantine Protocol (The "How")

To stop a mid-flow hijack, you cannot rely on willpower. Willpower is a battery that drains every time you hit "ignore" on a notification. Instead, we use **Physical Architecture**. We are going to build a literal, tangible wall between your "Deep Work" and your "Distracting Genius."

The Tangible Buffer

In Book 1, the Parking Lot was likely just a page in your planner. For the Thought Quarantine, we need something separate. Why? Because if you open your main planner or digital to-do list to write down an idea, you are exposing yourself to all your *other* tasks. You'll see that email you forgot to send or that bill that's due, and suddenly, you've traded one distraction for five.

The Quarantine requires **Tactile Isolation**. You need a stack of small Post-it notes, a scrap of paper, or a dedicated "Quarantine Notebook" that stays closed until the intruder arrives.

The "Catch, Fold, Drop" Ritual

This is the three-step mechanical process to clear your mental cache without breaking your flow.

1. **Catch**: The moment the thought hits—*"Wait, did I pay the registration for the car?"*—you write it down. Do not open a browser. Do not check your bank app. Just scribble the words. This honors the thought so your brain stops screaming about it, but it keeps your eyes on the "One-Screen Monogamy" of your current task.

2. **Fold**: This is the psychological "kill switch." Physically folding the paper or turning the page acts as a symbolic "closing of the file." You are telling your nervous system: *This is handled. It is no longer in my head; it is on the paper.*

3. **Drop**: You place that note into your **Quarantine Container**. This could be an old tea tin, a specific desk drawer, or even a literal envelope labeled "5:00 PM." By putting the thought in a container, you create a physical boundary. The thought is now in "time-out."

The Law of Grace for Your Nervous System

As a high-achiever—whether you are running a direct sales company or managing a legal practice—you know that time is money, but **focus is wealth**.

When you use the Quarantine Box, you aren't being "mean" to your ideas. You are practicing the Law of Grace. You are acknowledging that your brain is a "Shiny Object Specialist" and that it needs a safe place to store those objects so you can finish the work that actually pays the bills. You are protecting your nervous system from the frantic "ping-pong" of modern life.

By the time you drop that note into the tin, the urgency should drop by half. You've moved the problem from your "Internal RAM" to "External Storage." Now, you can get back to the Big Rock.

The 80% Rule & The 5:00 PM Review (The "Result")

Now comes the part where we prove your brain is a liar.

The biggest fear we have when a "brilliant" idea hits is **The Fear of Loss.** We think, *"If I don't look this up now, I'll forget the spark, and my business/case/life will suffer."* The Thought Quarantine is designed to test that theory using a time-delay.

The "Suspicious Cough" Tagline

In the legal world or in direct sales, if a lead or a piece of evidence looks shaky, you don't build your whole case on it immediately. You vet it. You should treat your mid-flow thoughts the same way.

Quarantine the thought like it has a suspicious cough—no visitors until the end of the day. By denying yourself the "immediate gratification" of a Google search or a LinkedIn update, you are forcing the thought to stand on its own merits.

The Expiration of Urgency

Here is the "No-BS" breakdown of what happens inside that Quarantine Box: **80% of the thoughts you put in there will lose their sparkle within four hours.**

When you open that tin at 5:00 p.m. (or during your "Distraction Autopsy" mentioned in Chapter 10), you will look at that pink Post-it that says *"REBRAND ENTIRE WEBSITE"* and realize it wasn't a brilliant business move—it was just a symptom of being bored with a spreadsheet at 10:42 a.m.

Why You Need Both (The Final Verdict)

You might ask, *"Is this redundant?"* Not a chance.

- **The Parking Lot** is your shield before the battle starts.

- **The Thought Quarantine** is your armor once you're in the middle of it.

Most people experience both patterns in a single day. You'll have a "shiny object" before breakfast (Parking Lot) and a self-sabotaging "research urge" mid-morning (Thought Quarantine). Having two slightly different tools stops the frustration of feeling like "nothing works." One tool catches the visitor; the other isolates the intruder.

Chapter 6 Action Step:

Find your container. It doesn't have to be fancy—a coffee mug, an old tea tin, or a dedicated desk drawer will do. For your next Ninety-Minute Fake Deadline, commit to the **"Write It & Forget It"** rule.

Scribble it. Fold it. Drop it.

Your future self (the one who actually finished the work) will thank you at 5:00 p.m. when they realize they didn't waste two hours on a LinkedIn banner that was actually "fine" all along.

Chapter 7 – The Boredom Tolerance Workout (Because Boredom Is A Muscle)

We have spent the last few chapters building a fortress around your focus. We've put the phone in physical exile, we've committed to "One-Screen Monogamy," and we've even built a "Quarantine Box" to trap those mid-flow hijacks.

But here is the uncomfortable truth: You can have the best tools in the world, but if your brain is terrified of a quiet room, you will eventually find a way to sabotage yourself.

Most of us treat boredom like a medical emergency. The second a webpage takes three seconds too long to load, or the person in front of us at the coffee shop takes too long to order their oat-milk latte, we reach for the "Glow." We don't even think about it. It's a reflexive twitch.

In this chapter, we aren't talking about "productivity hacks." We are talking about **Nervous System Weightlifting.** If you want to finish that book, close that deal, or finally draft that legal brief without feeling like your skin is crawling, you have to stop running from the "Quiet." You have to build a Boredom Callus.

The Dopamine Slot Machine (The "Why")

Think about the last time you stood in an elevator for four floors. What did you do? This phrase should be familiar to you Book 1 followers.

If you're like 99% of the population, you pulled out your phone. You didn't have a specific email to send. You didn't have a crisis to manage. You just couldn't handle the thirty-second "Analog Gap" between the lobby and your office.

We have effectively deleted the "Wait" from modern life. Between the microwave, the red light, and the bathroom break, we have filled every tiny crack of silence with a digital hit of dopamine.

The Death of the "Wait"

Your brain is a dopamine-seeking missile. It has been trained by the world's smartest engineers to believe that **New = Good** and **Quiet = Dangerous.** When you sit down to do "Deep Work," you are essentially asking a brain that is addicted to a 24/7 slot machine to suddenly enjoy watching paint dry. Of course it's going to scream. Of course it's going to tell you that checking your notifications is "urgent."

The Itch of the "Next Swipe"

This isn't a character flaw. It's a biological adaptation. Because we never let ourselves be bored, we've lost our "Boredom Tolerance."

When a task gets hard—when the proposal requires actual thinking or the research gets dry—your brain hits a "Boredom Wall." For a "Chronic Starter," this is the moment you usually bail. You tell yourself you need a "quick break," but what you're actually doing is feeding the addiction. You're telling your brain, *"Don't worry, if things get uncomfortable for even a second, I'll give you a hit of novelty."*

Boredom as a Warning Light

We need to flip the script. Boredom isn't a sign that the task is wrong; it's a "Low Battery" signal for your internal focus.

If you always plug that battery into a screen the second it dips, you never learn how to generate your own power. You remain a "Product of the Attention Economy". To become the person who actually finishes things, you have to learn to sit with the "Itch" without scratching it.

You have to realize that the "Magic Idea" you're looking for isn't in the next scroll—it's actually waiting for you on the other side of the boredom you're trying to avoid.

The Repetition Protocol (The "How")

If boredom is a muscle, then most of us are currently suffering from severe muscle atrophy. You can't go from scrolling TikTok for three hours a day to sitting in a silent room for an hour of deep work and expect it not to hurt. You have to start with **Progressive Resistance.**

We are going to rebuild your tolerance for "The Quiet" using the same logic a gym-goer uses to increase their bench press. We start small, we stay consistent, and we don't beat ourselves up when the "weight" feels heavy.

The "Micro-Wait" Exercise

The easiest place to start your workout is in the "Analog Gaps"—those tiny windows of time where nothing is happening. Usually, these are your biggest triggers for a "Quick Check."

Your mission: The next time you are waiting for the kettle to boil, standing in a lift, or waiting for a webpage to load, **do absolutely nothing.** Don't check the weather. Don't look at your "Sent" folder. Just stand there. Notice the "itch" to reach for your pocket. Feel the micro-panic of being "unstimulated." That feeling? That's the muscle growing.

The Three Levels of Boredom Weightlifting

To get serious, we need to move beyond the kettle and into intentional practice. Use these three levels to gauge your current "Focus Fitness":

- **Level 1: The Red Light Challenge**: When you're driving (a frequent haunt for us car commuters), and you hit a red light, keep your hands on the wheel and your eyes on the horizon. No podcasts, no skipping the song, and definitely no "sneaky" lap-checks. Just sit with the car.

- **Level 2: The Boring Three Minutes**: Set a timer on your oven (not your phone, we aren't inviting the devil to dinner) for three minutes. Sit in a chair. Look at a wall. Do not meditate. Do not try to be "zen." Just be bored. When your brain starts listing all the "productive" things you could be doing, remind it: *"We are training right now. This is the work."*

- **Level 3: The "Deep Rock" Stretch**: When you are in the middle of a Ninety-Minute Fake Deadline and you hit a wall of frustration or boredom, give yourself a **Five-Minute Buffer.** Tell yourself, *"I can use the Thought Quarantine in five minutes, but for the next 300 seconds, I am staying right here with this boring spreadsheet."*

The "One Less Refresh" Rule

As a business owner or a lawyer, you probably feel the need to be "on" at all times. But "on" usually just means "reactive." The Repetition Protocol isn't about becoming a monk; it's about the **One Less Refresh Rule.** If you usually refresh your emails ten times an hour, try for nine. If you check your LinkedIn Every time you finish a paragraph, try every two paragraphs.

We aren't looking for perfection; we are looking for **Internal Authority.** You are proving to your nervous system that *you* decide when the stimulation starts, not the notification light.

From Twitchy to Tough (The "Result")

If you stick with the Repetition Protocol, something strange starts to happen. The "micro-panic" you used to feel when standing in a lift without your phone begins to dissolve. You stop being a "twitchy" reactor and start becoming a "tough" observer.

This is the development of the **Boredom Callus**. Just like a guitarist's fingertips thicken so they can play longer without pain, your brain is thickening its ability to endure the "Quiet" without needing a digital rescue.

The Return of Creative Thought

As a direct sales leader or a legal professional, your value isn't just in your ability to "process" tasks—it's in your ability to think critically and creatively. But here's the problem: **Creative thoughts are shy.** They don't move into a house that is already packed with noisy guests.

When you scroll to "kill time," you are essentially evicting your best ideas before they can even unpack their bags. By building boredom tolerance, you are creating a "vacancy" in your mind. It is in those quiet, "boring" gaps—the shower, the walk to the car, the silent microwave wait—that your brain finally has the space to solve the problem that's been bugging you all week.

Building Internal Authority

The ultimate goal of this workout isn't to live a boring life; it's to regain **Internal Authority.** Right now, the "Attention Economy" owns your boredom. They have monetized your inability to sit still. When you choose to stay in the "Deep Rock" stretch for an extra five minutes, you are taking your power back. You are proving that you are a high-achiever who can handle the discomfort of the "Middle of the Task" just as well as the excitement of the "Start."

Chapter 7 Action Step:

The "Analog Afternoon" Challenge. Pick one activity this weekend—a walk in the park, a coffee at a cafe, or a meal—and leave the phone in **Physical**

Exile (Chapter 4). No podcasts, no "just in case" checks.

Chapter 8 – Planned Novelty Days (Scroll On Your Terms)

By now, you've spent a lot of time saying "no." No to the notification, no to the mid-task "brilliant" idea, and no to the immediate dopamine hit of the 10:42 a.m. ambush.

But let's be real: I am not a monk, and neither are you. You run a company, you manage a legal practice, and you live in the 21st century. You aren't going to delete the internet and move to a cabin in the woods (and even if you did, you'd probably just end up staring at a particularly interesting piece of moss for three hours).

We don't want to kill your curiosity; we just want to put a leash on it.

If you try to live in a state of permanent "Digital Celibacy," you are setting yourself up for a massive face-plant. This chapter is about the "Release Valve." It's about the moment you get to stop being a

"Recovering Chronic Starter" and just be a person who enjoys a good rabbit hole—on your own terms.

The Myth of Digital Celibacy (The "Why")

Most productivity books tell you that the internet is the enemy and that "true focus" means never looking at a meme again. That is a lie, and it's a dangerous one.

When you try to go "Cold Turkey" on novelty, you trigger what I call the **Rubber Band Effect.** You pull and pull and pull against your natural desire for stimulation, staying perfectly disciplined for three days. But that tension has to go somewhere. Eventually, the rubber band snaps, and you find yourself at 11:30 p.m. on a Tuesday night, deep-diving the Wikipedia page for "List of Unexplained Sounds" or watching "Restoration Videos" of 1950s rusty toy trucks.

Novelty is a Biological Need

Your "Shiny Object Specialist" brain isn't broken; it's actually a high-performance engine that thrives on new information. As a high-achiever, your curiosity is likely one of your greatest assets. It's what makes you good at sales and sharp in a courtroom.

The problem isn't the *content* you're consuming; it's the *lack of a schedule*. When you scroll "by accident," you are a victim. When you scroll "by design," you are a connoisseur.

From Accidental to Intentional

The **Planned Novelty Day** (or Window) is the psychological equivalent of a "Cheat Meal" in a fitness plan. If you know that you have full, guilt-free permission to spend Saturday afternoon in a YouTube vortex, your brain is much more likely to behave during your Tuesday morning "Deep Rock" session.

When the "Urge to Search" hits you mid-week, you can look at your *Thought Quarantine* tin and say, *"Not now, but definitely on Saturday."* This shifts your internal dialogue from "I'm not allowed to have fun" to "I'm saving the fun for the Sandbox."

By planning your novelty, you stop the "Shame Spiral." You move from the person who says, *"I was busy scrolling (and I hate myself),"* to the person who says, *"I am currently in my Novelty Window, and I am having a blast."* One is a trap; the other is a choice.

The Scheduled Sandbox (The "How")

To make this work, we have to stop treating the internet like a forbidden fruit and start treating it like a **Scheduled Sandbox**.

In a sandbox, there are no rules. You can dig, you can build, and you can throw sand (metaphorically). But the sandbox has wooden borders. It exists in a specific place and for a specific time. If you don't define the borders, the "sand" of the internet will eventually cover every inch of your house.

The "Saturday Morning Scroll"

The most effective way to implement this is to pick a "Vortex Window"—a block of time where you have full, executive permission to be as "unproductive" as you want.

For many high-achievers, this is a Saturday morning or a Sunday afternoon. During this window, the **One-Screen Monogamy** rule is suspended. You are allowed to have seventeen tabs open. You are allowed to follow the "Thought Quarantine" notes you collected all week. If you want to research "How to build a backyard pizza oven" for three hours even though you live in an apartment, this is your time.

The "Digital Cheat Meal" Logic

Think of this like a fitness plan. You stay disciplined during your "Ninety-Minute Fake Deadlines" on Tuesday because you know the Saturday Sandbox is coming.

When you're in the middle of a legal brief or a sales report and your brain screams, *"I wonder what that actor from that one show is doing now?"* you don't have to fight the thought with sheer willpower. You just tell your brain, *"That's a great question. We'll find out in the Sandbox on Saturday."* This lowers the internal tension immediately.

Setting the Boundary

To prevent the Sandbox from becoming a "Half-Day Trap," you need three simple guardrails:

1. **Define the Start**: Don't just "drift" into it. Make it an event. *"At 2:00 PM, I am entering the Sandbox."*

2. **Define the End**: Use a physical timer—like the one we used for your "Fake Deadlines." When the timer goes off, the Sandbox is closed. This prevents the "just one more video" loop that keeps you "Busy Scrolling" until 2:00 AM.

3. **The "No-Guilt" Rule**: This is the most important part. If you spend your Sandbox time feeling guilty about not working, you aren't resting; you're just procrastinating with a side of shame. **Permission is the point.** If you chose to be there, you aren't losing time—you're spending it.

By creating this "Digital Safety Zone," you prove to your nervous system that you aren't a prisoner of your own rules. You are the boss of your focus, and sometimes, the boss decides it's time for a break.

Reclaiming the Joy of the Internet (The "Result")

When you stop "sneaking" your scrolls, the internet actually starts being fun again.

Right now, your brain associates the "Notification Vortex" with a hangover—that gross, heavy feeling of realizing you just lost two hours to a strangers' home renovation and you're now behind on your billable hours. By implementing the Scheduled Sandbox, you move from **Accidental Consumption** to **Intentional Curation.**

The Law of Choice

In my life as a lawyer and a business owner, I am used to being the person in charge. But the algorithm is designed to take that power away. The Scheduled Sandbox is how you take it back.

There is a massive psychological difference between saying *"I was busy scrolling (and I'm a failure)"* and saying *"I am currently in my Saturday Sandbox, and I am choosing to watch this video about how to grow giant pumpkins."* One is a trap; the other is a luxury. When you choose the time and the place, the "Shame Gremlins" lose their power. You aren't "failing" at your workout plan or your work day—you are simply following the schedule you created for yourself.

Micro-Novelty vs. Macro-Novelty

Depending on how your "Shiny Object Specialist" brain works, you might need to adjust the dose:

- **The Macro-Novelty Day**: A long, 3-hour window on a Saturday (The "Full Sandbox"). Best for deep-dive researchers who need to feel like they've "finished" a rabbit hole.

- **The Micro-Novelty Window**: A 20-minute "release valve" at the end of every workday. Best for people who feel high levels of daily stress and need a small reward to transition from "Work Mode" to "Home Mode."

The "Guilt-Free" Finish Line

The ultimate result of Chapter 8 is that you stop living in a state of constant, low-grade anxiety about your phone. You know that the internet isn't going anywhere. You know that all those "Thought Quarantine" notes you've been collecting are safe in their tin, waiting for their moment in the sun.

When you reclaim the joy of the scroll, you stop being a "product" of the attention economy and start being a person who uses the world's information for their own entertainment. You've moved from being "busy scrolling" to being **right on time** for your own fun.

Chapter 8 Action Step:

Open your calendar right now. Find a block of time this weekend—at least 60 minutes—and label it **"THE SANDBOX."** During this time, the rules of the *Anti-Vortex Toolkit* are suspended. You have full permission to be "unproductive." But remember: the second that timer goes off, the sandbox is closed.

Chapter 9 – The Two-Minute Reset Ritual (When The Puppy Escapes Again)

Up until now, we've been operating under a "Laboratory Setting." We've talked about how to set up your desk, how to exile your phone, and how to build a "Quarantine Box" for your thoughts. In a perfect world, these tools would turn you into an unbreakable focus machine.

But you don't live in a laboratory.

You live in a world where the client calls with an "absolute emergency" three minutes into your Ninety-Minute Fake Deadline. You live in a house where the puppy literally escapes the yard and you have to spend twenty minutes chasing him through the neighbor's garden. You live in a human body that sometimes just *caves* and checks a notification at 11:00 a.m. because you're tired, hungry, or bored.

This chapter isn't about how to be perfect. It's about what to do when the wheels fall off. Because in the life of a high-achiever, the wheels **will** fall off. The question isn't whether you'll get distracted; it's how long it takes you to get back up. Now let's get a bit more science-y.

The "Puppy Escapes" Principle (The "Why")

There is a psychological trap that kills more productivity than TikTok ever could. I call it the **"All-or-Nothing" Tailspin.**

It looks like this: You planned to work from 9:00 a.m. to 10:30 a.m. At 9:15 a.m., something interrupts you—a phone call, a crying kid, or a moment of weakness where you "just checked one thing" and ended up in a twenty-minute vortex.

By 9:45 a.m., your brain starts whispering: *"Well, you've already ruined the morning. The 'Focus Block' is blown. You might as well just scroll until lunch and try again at 1:00 p.m."*

The Biscuit Logic

This is the same flawed logic that tells a person on a diet, *"I accidentally ate one biscuit, so I might as well eat the whole pack and the pizza."* As a lawyer and a business owner, you know that if a witness gives one bad answer, you don't just drop the whole case and walk out of the courtroom. You recalibrate. You pivot. You find a way to get the narrative back on track. Your workday deserves that same level of professional resilience.

The Grace of the Micro-Start

The "Puppy Escapes" Principle is a reminder that life is inherently messy. When the puppy escapes, you don't spend the rest of the day complaining about the fence; you catch the dog, put him back, and go back to what you were doing.

The "Reset" isn't a failure of the Anti-Vortex system; it is a **mandatory part of it.** You have to give yourself the Grace of the Micro-Start. You aren't "starting over" from zero, and you aren't a "failure" for losing forty minutes. You are simply a person living a real life who needs a two-minute ritual to tell their nervous system: *"The distraction is over. We are going back in now."*

Shortening the Recovery Time

Success in this book isn't measured by never being distracted. Success is measured by **Recovery Time.** *

The Old You: Gets distracted at 10:00 a.m., feels guilty, and writes off the day until "Monday."

- **The New You**: Gets distracted at 10:00 a.m., notices it at 10:15 a.m., performs a Two-Minute Reset, and is back in flow by 10:17 a.m.

We aren't chasing the ghost of a "Perfect You" who never fails. We are building a "Real You" who knows exactly how to wipe the blood off the floor and keep saving the life of their workday.

The Two-Minute Mechanical Reset (The "How")

When you realize you've been "Busy Scrolling" for twenty minutes, your brain is physically locked in a **Dopamine Loop**. You aren't just "procrastinating"; you are experiencing a physiological state where your prefrontal cortex (the boss of your brain) has been sidelined by the reward-seeking limbic system.

To get back to work, you can't just "think" your way out. You have to use a **Pattern Interrupter**. You need a mechanical reset that signals to your nervous system that the current "program" is over.

1. The Physical Shift (The Sensory Circuit-Breaker)

The first step is to move your body. Research in **Embodied Cognition** suggests that our physical state deeply influences our mental processes. A study published in *Psychological Science* found that even simple movements, like stretching or changing posture, can improve cognitive flexibility and help break "mental set" (the tendency to stick to a specific way of thinking or behaving) [Source: *Psychological Science*, "Body Posture Affects Confidence in One's Own Thoughts," 2009].

The Action: Stand up. Physically walk away from the screen—even if it's just three steps. Splash cold water on your face. This triggers the **Diving Reflex**, which instantly lowers your heart rate and resets the parasympathetic nervous system, pulling you out of the frantic "high-beta" brainwave state associated with digital overstimulation.

2. The "One-Rock" Declaration (Combatting Decision Fatigue)

When we snap out of a distraction, we often feel overwhelmed by the "mountain" of work we still have to do. This leads to **Decision Fatigue**, as we already know. This psychological phenomenon states where the more choices we have, the harder it is to make a good one [Source: *Journal of Personality and Social Psychology*, "Extrinsic Rewards and Implicit Motivation," Baumeister et al., 1998].

Instead of looking at your whole to-do list—which will likely send you running back to the "safety" of a scroll—you must pick **exactly one tiny task.**

The Action: Say it out loud: *"I am going to draft the first three sentences of this email."* By narrowing your focus to one "Micro-Rock," you bypass the brain's "threat response" to a large workload and rebuild your sense of **Self-Efficacy** (the belief in your ability to succeed).

3. The Breath of Permission (The Zeigarnik Reset)

The "All-or-Nothing" tailspin is fueled by **The Zeigarnik Effect**, as we keep on mentioning. If you carry the shame of the "lost hour" into your next task, your brain stays partially stuck in the past distraction.

The Action: Take one deep, four-second inhale and a six-second exhale. This "Extended Exhale" tells your Vagus nerve that there is no emergency. Mentally "close the file" on the distraction. You aren't a "failure" for the lost time; you are a professional performing a **Surgeon's Reset**.

The Surgeon's Mentality

In your life as a teacher, a professional, a parent, a whatever it is, you have to be the surgeon of your own day. A surgeon doesn't stop the operation because they dropped a tool or because there's blood on the floor; they perform a quick, sterile reset and keep going because **the life is still on the table.** In this case, the "life" is your focus, your goals, and your "Golden Hours." Don't let a twenty-minute "Puppy Escape" turn into a four-hour "Half-Day Trap." Perform the mechanical reset, pick up your "One Rock," and get back to work.

Self-Awareness Without the Shame (The "Result")

If you perform the Two-Minute Reset, something incredible happens: **The day starts over.** You don't have to wait for Monday. You don't even have to wait for the next hour. You are allowed to have a "Fresh Start" at 10:17 a.m. on a random Tuesday.

Shortening the Recovery Time

The true metric of success for a "Recovering Chronic Starter" isn't the absence of distraction—it's the **speed of the recovery.** Think back to the version of you who started this book. When that version of you got "Busy Scrolling," it usually meant the morning was gone. The guilt of the lost hour would snowball into a "Half-Day Trap," where you'd decide to "just catch up on admin" (which is code for checking emails and feeling busy without actually doing the Big Rock).

By using the Reset Ritual, you are shrinking that recovery time from four hours to two minutes. You are moving from a person who is *dragged* by their impulses to a person who simply *notices* them, resets, and moves on. This is what it means to have **Self-Awareness without the Shame.**

The "Real You" vs. The "Perfect You"

As a lawyer and a business owner, you spend a lot of time projecting an image of being "on top of it." You solve everyone else's problems. You are the one people turn to when things go wrong. But inside, when you find yourself in a 20-minute vortex of cat videos or LinkedIn banners, that "Golden Cage" of perfectionism can feel very heavy.

I want you to hear this clearly: **The "Perfect You" who never gets distracted doesn't exist.** That person is a ghost, and chasing them is what keeps you exhausted.

The "Real You"—the one who is currently reading these words—is much more impressive. The Real You is the one who has the courage to admit they've lost their way, the humility to splash some cold water on their face, and the grit to pick up that "One Rock" and keep going. That is where the real power lives. It's not in the "streak" of perfect days; it's in the collection of successful resets.

Chapter 9 Action Step:

Identify your "Reset Trigger." Decide right now what your physical "Pattern Interrupter" will be for the next time life gets messy. Will it be:

- A specific song that signals "Work Mode"?

- A physical stretch or three jumping jacks?
- A glass of ice-cold water?

Whatever it is, name it. The next time the "Puppy Escapes"—whether it's a literal dog or a metaphorical notification—don't look at the clock. Just trigger your reset, pick your One Rock, and be right on time for the next five minutes.

Chapter 10 – Distraction Autopsies (Turning "I Lost Two Hours" into "I Learned Something")

If you've followed the *Anti-Vortex Toolkit* this far, you are already ahead of 90% of the population (well not really the population – but perhaps 90% of others who are struggling with the notification vortex like us). You have the walls, the boxes, and the resets. But here is the reality of being a high-achiever: You are a sophisticated opponent. Your brain is smart enough to find the "cracks" in any system you build.

Eventually, you will have a "Face-Plant." You will find yourself staring at a screen, two hours deep into a rabbit hole, wondering where the morning went.

Most people respond to this with a "Shame Spiral." They beat themselves up, call themselves "lazy," and vow to "try harder" tomorrow. But "trying harder" is not a strategy. It's a prayer. In this chapter, we stop praying for discipline and start performing **Forensics.**

The Coroner's Mindset

When a high-value business deal collapses or a legal case takes an unexpected turn, you don't just sit in your office and cry about it. You perform a "Post-Mortem." You look at the evidence, the timeline, and the points of failure to ensure it never happens again.

Your focus deserves the same professional courtesy.

From Shame to Science

A "Face-Plant"—that moment you wake up from a two-hour scrolling trance—is not a character flaw; it is a **Data Point.** If you simply feel guilty, you learn nothing. You just carry a heavy backpack of shame into your next task, which actually makes you *more* likely to distract yourself again to escape the bad feeling.

But if you adopt the **Coroner's Mindset**, you treat those lost two hours like a cold case. You aren't "bad" for scrolling; your system just had a "Security Breach." The goal of a Distraction Autopsy is to find the **Cause of Death** for your productivity. Was it a "Sudden Trauma" (an unexpected phone call that broke your seal)? Or was it "Systemic Failure" (you were tired, hungry, and your phone was within arm's reach)?

The Weaponization of Self-Awareness

As a lawyer, you wouldn't walk into a courtroom without knowing the weaknesses in your own argument. As a business owner, you wouldn't launch a campaign without a "Failure Mode" analysis.

As a "Recovering Chronic Starter," you cannot win the war for your attention if you don't know exactly how you tend to lose it. When you remove the moral weight from your distractions, they stop being "failures" and start being **Intelligence Reports** from the front lines of your own mind. You aren't judging the victim; you're inspecting the crime scene so the next "break-in" is impossible.

The Forensic Protocol

To perform an effective autopsy, you cannot simply say, *"I got distracted."* That is like a coroner saying the cause of death was "the heart stopped beating." It's technically true, but it's useless for prevention.

To stop the next "Face-Plant," you need a specific framework. The next time you snap out of a "Vortex" and realize you've lost significant time, do not run to the next task immediately. Spend three minutes answering these **Three Forensic Questions**:

1. What was the "Entry Point"?

Every vortex starts with a single click—the "Gateway Drug."

- Was it a "suspiciously urgent" email that felt like work but was actually just noise?
- Was it a "quick check" of the weather that turned into a twenty-minute news scroll?
- Did you open LinkedIn "just to post" a business update and get tackled by the feed?

Identify the exact app or tab that acted as the "unlocked door" to your focus. In legal terms, this is your **Proximate Cause.**

2. What was the "Emotional State"?

Distraction is rarely about the content; it's about **Mood Regulation.** Research in the *Journal of Consumer Research* suggests that we are most vulnerable to impulsive behaviors when we are under "Cognitive Load"—basically, when our brains are tired or stressed [Source: Shiv & Fedorikhin, "Heart and Mind in Conflict," 1999].

Were you bored by a technical legal brief? Were you overwhelmed by a "Big Rock" task that felt too heavy to start? Or were you simply seeking a "Micro-Win" because you felt stuck? According to a study in *Self and Identity*, procrastination is a "coping mechanism for negative emotions," not a lack of time management [Source: Sirois & Pychyl, "Procrastination and the Priority of Short-Term Mood Regulation," 2013].

3. What was the "Friction Point"?

Where did the *Anti-Vortex Toolkit* fail?

- Was the phone in your pocket instead of **Physical Exile**?
- Did you forget to set your **Ninety-Minute Fake Deadline**?

- Was your "One-Screen Monogamy" rule broken by an "accidental" second tab?

Physical friction is the best predictor of behavior. If the "Glow" was too easy to reach, the system was rigged against you from the start. You didn't "fail"; the floor was just too slippery.

The "No-Judgment" Tally (The "Logic")

Information is only power if it is organized. In your legal practice, you look for "Precedent." In your marketing company, you look for "Consumer Trends." Your focus is no different.

Once you've performed a few autopsies, you will start to see the same "Entry Points" and "Friction Points" popping up. This is where you move from a **Coroner** to a **Security Consultant.** You need a simple, analog **Autopsy Log**—a dedicated page in your "Quarantine Notebook" where you keep a running tally of your "Face-Plants."

The Anatomy of the Tally

The goal here is **Data, not Drama.** You aren't writing a "Shame Diary" about how you failed; you are keeping a "Security Log." Every time you perform an autopsy, you add a tally mark next to the "Primary Cause."

After a week of being a "Recovering Chronic Starter," your log might look like this:

- **"Just Checking" Reflex**: | | | | (The door was left unlocked)

- **Overwhelmed by "Big Rock"**: | | (The task felt too heavy)

- **Physical Proximity to Phone**: | | | | | (The phone was in the room)

- **Tired/Low Blood Sugar**: | | | (The "Battery" was empty)

The Law of Patterns

If you see five tallies next to "Physical Proximity to Phone," the solution isn't "more willpower." As a lawyer, you know that if a specific intersection has ten accidents a week, you don't tell the drivers to "be better"; you install a traffic light.

By keeping a "No-Judgment Tally," you are building a **Security Patch** for your life. You are moving from the vague, heavy feeling of *"I keep failing"* to the sharp, actionable observation of *"I have identified a recurring glitch in the hardware, and I am now installing a fix."*

Separating the "Who" from the "How"

This is the most critical part of the logic: You are still a high-performer (the **Who**), even if your current system (the **How**) has a leak. When you see the tally marks, you aren't looking at your worth as a professional; you're looking at the efficiency of your toolkit.

A study on "Metacognitive Monitoring" suggests that people who track their errors without emotional attachment improve their performance significantly faster than those who simply "try harder" [Source: *Metacognition and Learning*, "The Role of Error Monitoring in Self-Regulated Learning," 2011]. You are weaponizing your mistakes to make yourself un-vortexable.

Patching the System (The "Result")

In your legal practice, if a specific contract clause keeps causing disputes, you don't just hope for better clients—you redraft the clause. In your marketing company, if a lead source is drying up, you don't just "work harder"—you reallocate the budget.

Section 4 is where you stop being a victim of your "Vortex" and start being the architect of your environment. This is **Data-Driven Defense.**

The "Hard-Patch" vs. The "Soft-Patch"

Once your **No-Judgment Tally** (Section 3) reveals a pattern, you apply one of two types of "patches":

1. **The Hard-Patch (Environmental)**: This is for when the data shows a "Proximity Failure." If you have five tally marks for "Phone was in the room," the Hard-Patch is simple: **Physical Exile** is no longer optional. You move the charging station to the kitchen. You don't negotiate with your willpower; you change the geography.

2. **The Soft-Patch (Process)**: This is for when the data shows an "Emotional Entry Point." If your autopsies show you "Face-Plant" every time you have to draft a complex affidavit, the Soft-Patch is to use a **Micro-Rock Declaration**. You tell yourself, *"I'm not writing the affidavit; I'm just listing the three key dates.*

The "High-Risk" Time Window

For most high-achievers in corporate worlds, the most dangerous time for a "Vortex" is between **3:00 PM and 4:30 PM**. This is when the "Decision Fatigue" from a day of legal battles and sales meetings peaks, and your blood sugar dips.

If your autopsies show a cluster of tallies in this window, don't fight it. **Patch it.** Schedule your **Planned Novelty Window** (Chapter 8) or a **Boredom Tolerance Workout** (Chapter 7) for exactly that time. You are preemptively releasing the pressure before the system blows.

The Reward of Self-Trust

The ultimate result of Chapter 10 isn't just a cleaner schedule; it's the return of **Self-Trust.** The reason most "Chronic Starters" feel anxious is that they never know *when* they are going to fall off the wagon. They feel like they are walking on thin ice.

But when you perform autopsies, the "boogeyman" of distraction loses its power. You stop wondering *if* you'll get distracted and start knowing exactly *why* it happens. You move from "I keep failing" to "I am currently optimizing my nervous system."

Success isn't a straight line; it's a series of "Reset Rituals" backed by "Forensic Data." You have turned your two-hour "Failure" into a "Security Upgrade" that will protect your next ten hours of Deep Work.

Chapter 10 Action Step:

The "Post-Mortem" Commitment. For the next seven days, every time you catch yourself in a vortex that lasts more than 15 minutes, you are legally required (by the rules of this book) to perform a **Three-Question Autopsy.** Do not skip it. The data you gather this week is more valuable than any "productivity hack" on the planet.

Chapter 11: The Surgeon's Close (Your First 30 Days)

You have the toolkit. You have the "Exile" protocols for your phone, the "Fake Deadlines" for your ego, and the "Forensic Autopsies" for your failures. But as a lawyer and a business owner, you know that a contract is only as good as its execution.

This final chapter is the "Stitch." It's where we close the wound of chronic distraction and ensure that the "Recovering Chronic Starter" doesn't just have a good week, but a transformed career. We aren't looking for a "productivity spike"; we are looking for a permanent shift in your internal operating system.

The 30-Day Identity Shift (The Internal)

The most dangerous part of any new system is the "Dip"—the first 72 to 96 hours where the novelty wears off and the "itch" for the Glow becomes a physical ache. Because you are a high-achiever, your brain is incredibly skilled at **Intellectualized Procrastination.** It will try to "negotiate" with you. It will tell you that a client might be emailing an emergency or that you're missing a critical update in your direct sales funnel.

The Focus Hangover

You must treat the first 30 days as a clinical trial. Your brain is currently addicted to the "Micro-Hits" of dopamine provided by the Vortex. When you switch to **Single-Screen Monogamy** and **Physical Exile**, you are going into withdrawal.

Expect to feel "boring." Expect to feel like you're moving slower than the rest of the world. This is the **Focus Hangover.** It is the feeling of your prefrontal cortex waking up from a long, digital slumber.

The Identity Rebrand

Stop saying, *"I'm trying to be less distracted."* That is the language of a victim. Start saying, **"I am a high-performer who protects my attention."** In the courtroom, the "burden of proof" is on the prosecution. In your own mind, the burden of proof is on your actions. Every time you finish a **Ninety-Minute Fake Deadline** without checking your phone, you are submitting "Exhibit A" to your own brain that the "New You" is the one in charge.

The Boredom Callus (The 30-Day Rule)

Neurologically, it takes roughly 21 to 30 days to weaken an old neural pathway and strengthen a new one. By Day 14, the "panic" of not having your phone on your desk will fade. By Day 30, sitting in a silent room to think through a complex legal strategy won't feel like a chore; it will feel like a **competitive advantage.** You are building a **Boredom Callus** so thick that the "noise" of the internet can no longer pierce your skin. You aren't "missing out" on the world; you are finally present enough to dominate your corner of it.

The CEO's Operating System (The External)

Now that you've patched your own system, you have to protect it from the world. In the fast-paced business culture of QLD, "availability" is often mistaken for "productivity." If you are always reachable, you are never deep. To stay **Un-Vortexable** long-term, you must turn these tools into a permanent **Maintenance Schedule**.

1. The Sunday "War Room" Prep

You wouldn't walk into a complex litigation without a strategy; don't walk into your work week without a map. Every Sunday night (or Monday morning before the "Glow" starts), spend 15 minutes in your **Quarantine Notebook**.

- **Block the Rocks**: Physically draw out your **Ninety-Minute Fake Deadlines** for the week.
- **The Novelty Release Valve**: Pre-schedule your **Planned Novelty Windows** (Chapter 8). If you

don't decide *when* the fun happens, the Vortex will decide for you at 2:00 PM on a Tuesday.

- **The Audit**: Look at your **Autopsy Tally** from the previous week. If you "Face-Planted" three times because your phone was in the room, the Sunday "War Room" is where you commit to a stricter **Physical Exile** protocol.

2. Leading the Un-Vortexable Team

As a business owner and a lawyer, your focus (or lack thereof) sets the "weather" for everyone else. You need to scale this culture so your staff isn't accidentally pulling you back into the Vortex.

- **The "Deep Rock" Signal**: Create a physical or digital signal that tells your team: *"When this light is on (or my door is shut), I am in a Fake Deadline. Unless the building is literally on fire, do not breach the seal."*

- **The "Asynchronous" Law**: Encourage your team to use "Thought Quarantine" for you. Instead of "Quick Questions" that ruin your flow, have them batch their queries for a 15-minute sync at the end of the day. You are protecting their attention as much as your own.

3. The Self-Respect Dividend (The "Result")

The ultimate result of the *Anti-Vortex Toolkit* isn't just a cleaner schedule; it is the return of your **Self-Respect**. There is a quiet, powerful confidence that comes from knowing you finished your "Big Rocks" by 11:00 AM.

When the workday is structured this way, you aren't just "productive"—you're free. You can hit the gym for **Training Plan 1**, focus on high-level strategy for your direct sales company, or head home early to be fully present with your family. You no longer have "Guilt Gremlins" whispering in your ear because you know, with forensic certainty, that the work is done.

The Final Action Step: The Surgeon's Oath

To close the book, I want you to write this one sentence on a post-it note and stick it to the corner of your monitor. It is your "Standing Order":

"My focus is my most valuable asset. I decide when the stimulation starts, and I decide when the work is done."

For a long time, you might have felt like a passenger in your own brain, pulled along by every notification and "urgent" whim. But through these eleven chapters, you've done something most people never will: you've reclaimed the **Internal Authority** required to be a true closer.

QUICK REFERECE ANTI-VORTEX SHEET

(The Most Important or Most Ignored Page)

I. The Golden Rule of Environment

- **Physical Exile**: If the phone is in the room, the system is broken. During "Big Rock" blocks, the "Glow" lives in a drawer, a bag, or another room.

- **One-Screen Monogamy**: One monitor, one tab, one task. If you need to research, do it in a timed "Sandbox" later.

- **The Quarantine Box**: Keep a physical notebook (The Tin) next to your keyboard. Every "urgent" random thought goes in the box, not in a new browser tab.

II. The Execution Protocol (The 90-Minute Sprint)

1. **Declare the "Big Rock"**: Write down exactly one high-value task.
2. **Set the Fake Deadline**: Set a physical timer for **90 minutes**. This is your "Surgery." The seal cannot be breached.
3. **The Boredom Callus**: When you hit a wall, do not click away. Sit with the boredom for **2 minutes**. The breakthrough is on the other side of that itch.

III. The Emergency "Reset Ritual"

When the "Puppy Escapes" (you get distracted or interrupted):

1. **Pattern Interrupt**: Stand up, stretch, or splash cold water on your face.
2. **The One-Rock Declaration**: Say out loud: *"I am now doing [One Tiny Task] for five minutes."*
3. **The Extended Exhale**: One deep breath. Forgive the lost time. The day starts over **now**.

IV. The Maintenance Schedule

- **Sunday "War Room"**: Map your "Fake Deadlines" for the week.

- **Planned Novelty (The Sandbox)**: Schedule 60 minutes of "Guilt-Free Scrolling" on Saturday. If it's scheduled, it's a luxury; if it's accidental, it's a trap.

- **The Distraction Autopsy**: If you lose an hour, ask: *What was the entry point? What was the friction point?* Update the system, don't blame the person.

V. The Surgeon's Oath

"My focus is my most valuable asset. I decide when the stimulation starts, and I decide when the work is done. I am the closer."

Prologue – A Final Nudge (No Pep Talks)

(You have reached the end – good on you! Proud person over here)

You didn't buy this book for a pep talk. You've had enough of those. You've watched the "Rise and Grind" videos, you've bought the $60 planners that now sit empty in your desk drawer, and you've told yourself "tomorrow is the day" more times than you can count.

If pep talks worked, you'd be the most productive person in Queensland by now.

The problem isn't your motivation; it's your biology. You are a high-achiever with a brain that is literally too smart for its own good. You've spent years building a business and a legal career by being a "Starter"—someone who can spot an opportunity and jump. But that same "start-up" energy is exactly what the algorithm uses to hijack your day.

This book wasn't written to make you feel better about yourself. It was written to give you a **Manual for the Hardware.** As you turn this page, remember: The "Vortex" is a billion-dollar industry designed to keep you scrolling. You cannot beat a billion-dollar industry with "willpower." You beat it with systems. You beat it with **Physical Exile, Fake Deadlines**, and the **Surgeon's Reset**.

The surgery is about to begin. Don't look for inspiration. Look for the timer.

—I.L. Hartley

Recovering Chronic Starter

The End.

www.ingramcontent.com/pod-product-compliance
Lightning Source LLC
Chambersburg PA
CBHW050948050726
47592CB00007B/2477